While every precaution has been
book, the publisher assumes no 1
sions, or for damages resulting from the use of the information
contained herein.

POWER TO TRAIL AND ULTRA RUNNERS

Second edition. May 27, 2023.

Copyright © 2023 Dr. Markus Holler

Written by Dr. Markus Holler.

1 - Introduction 4
2 - Running-Power Physics 7
2.1 Power and Running 7
2.2 Measuring Running Power 14
2.3 Flat Running 21
2.4 Uphill 25
2.5 Downhill 28
2.6 Trail Running 30
2.7 Concluding Overview 31
3 - Important Metrics 34
3.1 Functional Threshold Power 34
3.2 Power Zones 37
3.3 Workout Metrics 41
4 - Training Foundation 56
4.1 Power and Heart Rate 56
4.2 Using Power Metrics for Training 65
5 - Race Preparation 75
5.1 Setting The Goal 77
5.2 Preparing 93
5.3 Race Strategy 103

5.4 On Race Day 108

5.5 Summary 109

6 - Workouts and Training Plans 111

6.1 Key Workouts 111

6.2 Setting up a Training Plan 120

6.3 Example Training Plan - 8 Weeks Preparation and 3.5 h Race Duration 126

6.4 Example Training Plan - 12 Weeks Preparation and 10 h Race Duration.................................132

References..140

Appendix: Running Power Meters.....142

Glossary..144

1 - INTRODUCTION

Running belongs to the very fundamental types of human locomotion. It appears so natural to us that one might expect we would by now have reached a state where we have learned everything about it. But that is not the case. There is still lots of ongoing research about various aspects of running, and new measurements keep improving the training quality of both elite runners and amateurs. In cycling, such a new measurement effectively revolutionized the training, starting a few decades ago. The calculated quantity objectifies the mechanical effort of an athlete, a physical insight that considerably improved steering the intensity both during workouts and races. This seemingly revolutionary measurand actually corresponds to one of the most basic physical concepts: Power.

Given the immense success of Power meters in cycling, it may at first appear peculiar that the same didn't happen right afterwards in the sports of running. The reason is that while conducting such a measurement on a bike is relatively straightforward, measuring the Power output of a runner is considerably more complicated. Solutions that provided usable results just started to appear in recent years, and their development stage is certainly not yet finished. Following the release of the first running Power meters, the first books that focused on exploiting this newly available data for training and racing were published soon after. However, the currently available literature is primarily written for road runners whose maximum racing goal is a marathon, which leaves out trail, mountain, and ultra runners. Power-based training and racing also have a huge potential in these fields of running, but exploiting them needs a different approach. Given that each trail race is unique and can hardly be compared with others, training methods that are optimized for road running with its standardized race distances are hardly applicable here. Instead, I specifically developed an adaptive, Power-based concept to optimally train for and conduct any specific trail or ultra race. Covering the specifics of Power-based running for those enjoying trails and long distances also implies introducing new quantities, which are by nature not yet generally available. However, I've ensured that everything that is necessary for successful training and racing is not only possible with different types of Power meters but even illustrated in a way such that the training analysis can be carried out without additional costs.

All illustrations of Power data that are going to follow are based on results obtained with a Power-meter solution that I developed myself (see Appendix). Despite that, the aim is to provide a general guide to using Power meters for trail and ultra running, and therefore one of the main goals was to be as objective as possible. The whole topic of Power-based running is admittedly rather technical. Still, just as with other technological devices, that doesn't mean you have to be an expert and understand every detail to benefit from using it. For better understanding, technical aspects and calculations are illustrated with examples whenever possible, hopefully making this book a standard reference for many ambitious runners.

2 - RUNNING-POWER PHYSICS

If you already own a running Power meter, you are probably eager to find out right away how to use it for your training, and that is completely understandable. However, we first have to lay the groundwork, and this is what this chapter is about. It starts with a short excursion regarding the physical basics of Power and its relation to running, followed by an overview of the different types of Power meters. After that, the influence of various terrain types on the measured Power is explained.

In case you find this chapter complicated to read, do not hesitate to jump over the technical sections (or maybe directly to the next one). You should still be able to follow the rest of the book without the corresponding knowledge.

2.1 POWER AND RUNNING

Before we dive in detail into the different running conditions relevant for trail and ultra running, it is first necessary to introduce some physical foundations. To understand what Power is, we first need another physical quantity: Work (generally abbreviated to *W*). There are different types of work, and they can principally be converted into each other. However, we will focus on the one which is most important for us, namely *mechanical* work. It is defined as the multiplication of a force F that is applied along a direction and the distance moved in that direction, Δd:

$$\Delta W = F \cdot \Delta d.$$

As an example, think about lifting an object, say a clean plate you want to move from a table up to its cupboard: The gravity of the Earth drags it downwards, but as long as it is on the table, there is no movement, hence $\Delta d = 0$ and thus also ΔW. Now you lift it up - to do so, you have to apply an upward force to (over)compensate the gravitational force. By multiplying that force with the height difference between the table and the cupboard, you get the corresponding mechanical work. If you accidentally drop the plate near the top, the whole process is reversed. Suddenly your compensating force is missing, and what remains is the gravitational force that pulls the plate towards the Earth. In that situation, the gravitational field exerts work on the plate until it is stopped by an obstacle (hopefully not your foot).

With the concept of work, we almost have what we want - a quantity that objectively describes the physical load corresponding to a movement. There is only one piece missing, which is time. This is where the Power P comes in. It corresponds to the amount of work ΔW that is exerted per unit of time Δt, or alternatively the force in the direction of movement times the corresponding velocity v:

$$P = \frac{\Delta W}{\Delta t} = F \cdot v$$

Going back to our example, this means that the Power during plate-lifting is twice as high when you lift it in half the amount of time, or alternatively take two plates at once (as this means doubling the force). The choice of units for F, Δd, and Δt determine the resulting unit of P. In our context, the standard unit for P is Watt (abbreviated to W, not to be confused with the abbreviation of the work W). Keeping our definitions of work and Power in mind, 1 Watt is defined as follows:

$$1\,\text{Watt} = \frac{\text{Newton} \cdot \text{meter}}{\text{second}},$$

which means that if you apply a force of 1 Newton to an object and move it in that direction with 1 meter per second, the corresponding Power is 1 Watt. Now you might understandably wonder what 1 Newton is. Instead of taking the nominal definition, let us go back to the gravitational force. Anywhere on Earth, the gravitational force F_g of an object with a certain mass m in units of kilogram is

$$F_g[\text{Newton}] = 9.8 \cdot m[\text{kg}].$$

For illustration, we now leave the kitchen and take a running-related example. According to the last equation, the gravitational force of a runner with $m = 70\,\text{kg}$ is $F_g = 686\,\text{Newton}$. Running up a mountain with a vertical speed of $800\,\frac{\text{meter}}{\text{hour}} = 0.22\,\frac{\text{meter}}{\text{second}}$, the mechanical Power to work against the gravitational force is

$$P_g = 686\,\text{Newton} \cdot 0.22\,\frac{\text{meter}}{\text{second}} = 151\,\text{W}.$$

This is not the only component relevant for uphill running but, for larger inclinations, the most important one - more about that in the dedicated section of this chapter. If the runner now increases P_g, the vertical speed increases correspondingly, illustrating the general suitability of Power to be used as a live training metric. In contrast, the gravitational work performed during the ascent is independent of the vertical speed or total duration.

Thinking back on the definition of work - the multiplication of a force F *along a direction* and the distance moved *in that direction* Δd - you might start to wonder if it even makes sense to use Power for horizontal running. After all, there is usually no horizontal force to work against, and hence the work (and therefore Power) associated with a movement in any horizontal direction would be 0. That way of argumentation is widespread in physics education when introducing work and Power, and maybe you even recall having heard it back in school. However, reflecting on how tiring your running workouts sometimes are, you likely realize that something must be wrong with it. That becomes even more obvious when you think about cycling (see also Figure 2.1).

During pedaling, you work against a resistive force and move the pedal in the corresponding direction (which is constantly changing as it is a circular motion), so there the Power is obviously non-zero. If riding at a constant velocity on a flat road, this Power compensates for friction from the airstream as well as the tires. Now you see where the problem with this *"there is no work/Power for horizontal*

Figure 2.1: Schematic illustration of Power-related motions for cycling and running. For cycling, only one force-velocity pair is drawn, corresponding to the main Power component measured by the Power meter. In the case of running, many individual motions contribute to the overall Power, where just a few are shown.

movements" argumentation lies: It is valid under very simplistic conditions (no friction) but totally neglects the complexity of reality. So how is Power involved in horizontal running? At the very end, the answer is the same as for cycling - all your Power is eventually converted into friction - which, although it is correct, is not really helpful.

What we instead want is the running analogy to pedaling, i.e., the processes with mechanical Power involved that maintain the forward motion and thus compensate friction. Although the sum of these processes is far more complicated than turning a pedal, a schematic comprehension is luckily possible without a full biomechanical analysis. The keys to understanding an essential fraction of the Power of the running motion are acceleration and (again) gravitational work. Whenever an object is accelerated, there is a force that accelerates it, and together with the corresponding change of distance, this means that there is Power. Even when running at a constant speed, you continuously accelerate your limbs and rotate your core and upper body - which also implies acceleration - to maintain the forward motion. While a part of the force delivered by the muscles is used for acceleration, another large fraction is converted into gravitational Power of the limbs (for example, when lifting the legs), and these components are also partly converted into each other.

In the end, the purpose of all these efforts is to generate an effective stride that also involves other components of Power, such as the one corresponding to vertical oscillation (more about that later). However, it is important to realize that part of the Power your muscles provide is directly used for all these various acceleration and lifting/gravitational-work processes, and a certain fraction of that is lost to body-internal friction. You don't believe me? Then let's do a quick test. Maybe you already know and carry out heel flicks, i.e., alternate leg kicks up behind your body to reach your glutes, as part of your warm-up routine. They are typically executed in a slightly jumping manner to enable quicker alternations that we will avoid because of the apparent gravitational work you exert on your total body. So just perform the flicks from a standing position, meaning that you quickly lift one lower leg to your glutes and then down again, directly followed by the other one. When doing many of these in a row while wearing a heart-rate monitor (ideally with a chest strap for better accuracy), you should observe how your heart rises - by how much depends on your training level and the alternation frequency. Nevertheless, the fact that it increases means that the motion involves Power. When you think about it, you see that this type of motion involves gravitational work but also acceleration. The flicks notably correspond to an isolated part of the overall running process, except that the upward movement usually doesn't extend that far. The relevant point is that all the individual motions you perform while running contribute to the overall Power. Ideally, all these components would be measured and adequately considered by the Power meter you use.

While our muscles, tendons, and ligaments do a great job in storing and again releasing part of the corresponding energy, the whole movement comes at the cost of friction. When thinking about friction, what usually comes to mind is external friction related to the touching of surfaces in relative motion, such as the tires of your bicycle or your shoes on the ground. All that is certainly relevant, but there is another type of friction during sports, namely body-internal muscular friction. Running involves various muscles to deliver force and thus Power, and part of that Power is converted to internal energy, namely heat. Not really efficient, you say? You are definitely right! Just think about how easy it would be even for a mediocre-trained person to cover the distance of a (flat) marathon on a proper bicycle faster than the world's best runners can on their feet. From that perspective, running on flat terrain is a very inefficient way of locomotion, especially compared to cycling. That's a rather pessimistic statement, but it also means that there are several possibilities to become a faster runner. While for cyclists the main goal is to increase their Power (or Power per body mass) output, as a runner it is very beneficial to increase the efficiency of the overall running process to minimize the amount of unnecessarily spent Power as much as possible.

2.2 MEASURING RUNNING POWER

As we have just seen, running Power involves many different components, which makes an accurate measurement very complicated. Let's again take cycling for comparison: Given the fairly simple movement where the upper body is ideally motionless, reducing the Power measurement to the pedaling is perfectly fine. If the cyclist moves their upper body (maybe inadvertently because of poor posture or exhaustion), this implies an additional contribution not recorded by the Power meter. However, that is generally not a significant problem because this component is usually negligible. Furthermore, the cyclist is aware that the device only measures the pedaling Power. The leg movement is strongly associated with the pedaling cycle and, therefore, mainly contributes to it. Nonetheless, a part of it is lost to muscular friction and thus never reaches the pedal. Compared to running, however, this component plays a minor role. For a given athlete and cadence, it is constant and therefore acts as an offset of the measured value, which can be considered unproblematic if not too high. As already indicated in the previous section, a direct measurement of the pedaling Power is conducted by measuring the deployed force and multiplying it with the rotational velocity. In reality, many cycling Power meters nowadays work indirectly, meaning that they exploit the correlation of the pedaling Power with other quantities and only measure the latter. This approach may sound a bit like cheating, but what counts in the end is the achieved accuracy of the applied method.

So how can we now measure running Power? As we have seen, the simplifications assumed for the calculation of cycling Power are not really transferable to running. For an accurate and ideal calculation, all relevant forces and motions would be measured and properly combined. It is evident that this is not how current running Power meters work. Similar to corresponding devices for cycling, some measure either part of the involved Power, whereas others rely on its correlation to other measurable quantities. Let's take a look at the currently available types of running Power meters. Some specific Power meters are listed in the Appendix.

Direct Force Power Meters

This type is the running analogy to cycling Power meters. It tries to directly measure running Power, usually with insoles, by determining the forces during ground contact. With the previous considerations in mind, it is clear that this approach neglects all the other components (leg movement during flight phase, upper body, etc.).

Acceleration-Sensor Power Meters

Running Power meters of this type use a small sensor to measure acceleration in (ideally) all three spatial directions. It is typically applied to one of the shoes. With the knowledge of the runner's weight, the measurement of the acceleration of the corresponding foot allows deriving a Power number. That implies that the calculation assumes a particular distribution of the weight to different body parts. Furthermore, the measurement naturally doesn't include the upper body. Nevertheless, the complete continuous mapping of the foot's motion allows a relatively stable measurement. In addition, variables related to the runner's efficiency can be determined. Another advantage is the possibility to measure wind speed (including weather wind) directly with the sensor, whereas other approaches have to rely on indirect sources of information. This type of device is currently the most widespread. Disadvantages are the comparably high price and the fact that you need to make sure always to attach it to the shoe you are wearing.

Watch-Based Power Meters

Given the increasing interest among runners in using Power as a training metric, some sports-watch brands have begun to integrate corresponding calculations into their recent higher-end models, a trend that will undoubtedly continue. The immediate advantage is clear: You need a sports watch to display the Power anyway (I'm just assuming you do because you're reading this book), and if it already comes with a built-in calculation, then you don't need to buy yet another device. For watches without this integrated feature but with the possibility of installing additional apps or data fields, similar solutions are provided by third-party developers. A watch-based running-Power estimate combines watch-internal data, like cadence and vertical speed from the barometric altimeter, with external data, such as the velocity calculated from satellite information or the wind speed and orientation received from a nearby weather station. This corresponds to a less direct measurement compared to sensor-based approaches. Velocities derived from satellite information or the barometric altimeter are typically prone to inaccuracies as well as time lags of the order of a few seconds, implying a corresponding delay of derived quantities like Power. Although such time lags are certainly disadvantageous, they might be acceptable to many users, especially since it is generally advisable to display the average Power of the past few seconds (at least) to smooth out fluctuations.

"Hybrid" Power Meters

This category builds upon the previous one. A few watch-based solutions aim to increase accuracy by using additional data from acceleration sensors, corresponding to a "hybrid" approach between the acceleration-sensor and watch-based types. The sensor doesn't necessarily have to be a dedicated unit. What has instead become quite common nowadays are heart-rate belts with integrated acceleration sensors, providing instantaneous running-related information such as vertical oscillation (i.e., jump height) or ground contact time. The complementary data allows for improving the calculation in general as well as deriving other quantities, such as a simple estimate of running efficiency. However, as of 2022 and after that, some major brands have begun to calculate vertical oscillation and ground contact time directly on the watch by evaluating the arm movement. These developments allow for improved Power calculation without external sensors.

General Considerations on Power Meters

If you haven't yet decided on a specific type/approach, you'll likely wonder what you should get now. Currently, the market is dominated by one particular acceleration sensor. When searching for it on the internet, the marketing behind it will put in great effort to convince you that this is the best way to go. I'm not saying you shouldn't buy one, but maybe check the other options before doing so. Perhaps for your use case, you might also be satisfied with another solution and additionally save quite some money as well. Especially watch-based/hybrid approaches are interesting alternatives for many athletes.

Accuracy and Ways of Counting Power

Although the vendor of your product will very likely try to convince you of the opposite, measuring running Power is (at least today) no exact science. While some devices might work more reliably than others, there is not one specific and correct way of deriving a Power number. There are different opinions and approaches on how to do that, and even if someone has good reasons to go for a specific one, that still doesn't mean that the others are per se incorrect. In addition, the fact that all current devices only measure part of the overall motion implies that the rest of it is either estimated or ignored. That being said, the Power meter you've chosen might still provide precise numbers under varying conditions, enabling you to boost both your training and racing to a new level. Just remember not to trust it blindly, and don't expect different types to yield compatible results. A large part of this discrepancy between different approaches comes from diverging opinions on how to sum up the contributing components and how to deal with elastic energy. What does that mean? For example, during flat running (see the following section), you lift your body by a few centimeters with each step, exerting Power which is converted into gravitational energy. When the jump height is measured, this Power component can be calculated. The straightforward way of combining it with the rest would be just to add it, as is done by some algorithms. However, studies using force-measuring treadmills (see the survey by Snyder, Kram, and Gottschall, reference 1) have shown that a considerable fraction of the corresponding energy is elastically stored and reused by our muscles during impact. Taking this into account during the calculation makes a lot of sense (you see which approach I'm in favor of) as it avoids double-counting Power and is thus better correlated with our metabolic energy supply. But as just said, this doesn't mean that the former approach is wrong.

Keeping all this in mind, we will now discuss different running conditions and the involved Power components. The considerations and calculations underlying this discussion are based on a semi-analytical physical model that was developed for my own watch-based/hybrid Power meter (see Appendix). This means that the components behind the final Power number are all physically motivated, but some of its parameters are adjusted to yield reasonable results, as has been calibrated with a cycling Power meter. With this approach, the variety of different motions is grouped into different categories, which are easier to grasp and can be calculated and displayed as functions of quantities like running velocity.

2.3 FLAT RUNNING

When running in flat, non-technical terrain, the exerted Power can be categorized into the components outlined below. Please keep in mind that this scheme reflects a specific choice of calculating the various components. The contributions together with the total Power are illustrated as a function of running velocity in Figure 2.2.

Vertical Power

As already briefly mentioned before, each stride marks the beginning of a small jump, which distinguishes running from walking. This jump is necessary for a flight phase, which enables moving at a higher speed than when just setting one foot in front of the other, i.e., walking. The vertical Power for a given stride can be calculated if the jump height (also called vertical oscillation) is measured, which needs to be combined with the cadence as well as the runner's weight and the assumed elasticity factor. The latter depends on many parameters and is usually hard to determine from the available data, but without inclination, it should (again following reference 1) in most cases be around 50%. Typical values of the vertical oscillation range between 7 and 11 cm and vary from runner to runner, but generally also depend on speed and inclination. In Figure 2.2, no velocity dependency of the vertical oscillation is assumed, a simplification that is not valid for all runners but still doesn't heavily distort the functional relation for those where it is not. The

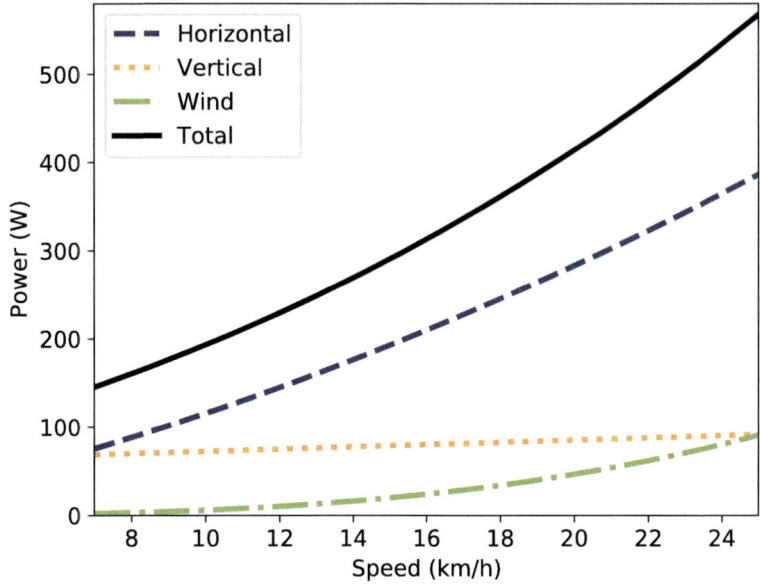

Figure 2.2: Contributions of different Power components during flat running for a runner with a bodyweight of 72 kg and height 184 cm as a function of running speed.

resulting vertical Power only rises slightly for higher velocities because of an increased cadence. We can therefore consider it as a fundamental component of running; in a way, it is like the necessary baseline to retain the process. Running Power in general increases considerably with higher speeds, but percentage-wise the contribution of Vertical Power decreases. This knowledge can serve as quite a good motivation for beginners who want to become faster: Apart from improving running efficiency or losing weight, the straightforward way to achieve this goal is to improve the overall fitness and thus increase the Power output. The fact that vertical Power is almost velocity-independent means that the largest part of the gain directly contributes to components related to forward motion.

Horizontal Power

In this context, horizontal Power refers to the combination of components that are necessary to maintain a given speed, leaving the influence of wind (both airflow and weather-related) aside. This encompasses the majority of forces and motions mentioned earlier, such as the movement of your legs and arms, the rotation of your upper body, as well as mechanical friction lost during ground contact. This Power component is also drawn for the exemplary runner in Figure 2.2. It rises with increasing velocity, and according to the model used here, it does so even faster than the velocity itself. This behavior is visible by the bending of the dashed blue line.

There is a physical motivation behind that functional relation. As we have schematically discussed before, the motions that fall into this category correspond to different types of Power. Lifting your legs, for example, relates to gravitational Power, which depends linearly on velocity (i.e., there's no bending of the function for this type in case the cadence stays the same). The components that are related to acceleration, however, show different behavior: When running faster, the range and velocity of the performed motions are typically larger, even (or especially) when the cadence is kept constant. The increase in Power is not linear anymore but rises faster. Perhaps you have already experienced this effect. During an easy run, the motion of the upper body usually comes automatically without much additional effort. However, you likely noticed how much your upper body has to work when running a very fast sprint. Keeping this in mind, it also makes sense why short-distance sprinters generally have quite muscular upper bodies. If that weren't needed and only the leg Power of the athlete would count, the fastest sprinters would surely look different.

Wind-Related Power

Compared to cycling, the influence of wind is probably estimated to be negligible by many runners. In case only the airflow from the runner's motion has to be considered (i.e., when it's windless), the corresponding contribution to the overall Power is indeed rather low for easy and moderate paces (see again Figure 2.2). That changes drastically for higher speeds, and as opposed to some other Power components, the functional relation is well known to be cubical in this case. This means that doubling the velocity increases the wind-related Power by a factor of eight. The contribution still appears comparably small, but that quickly changes in case of a headwind. For an arbitrary wind bearing, only the part that is parallel to the directional movement plays a major role, which has to be added to the proper motion. That way, a frontal headwind of, e.g., 15 km/h and a running speed of 10 km/h (pace 6 min/km respectively 9:40

min/mi) correspond to an effective airflow of 25 km/h. So while you're still running at 10 km/h, you have to put in considerably more effort.

2.4 UPHILL

If we'd always run on perfectly flat terrain such as a track, the benefits of using a Power meter over pace-based training would honestly be moderate. Sure, if it takes wind properly into account, you gain some accuracy, and you could try to use it to improve your running efficiency. But in principle, you wouldn't gain much from Power-based training compared to a well-prepared pace-oriented plan in this case. However, most of us don't carry out our runs entirely on flat terrain, and if you're a trail runner, then the chances are high that many of your runs even cover lots of altitude differences. Pace obviously fails as a training metric in this case, whereas Power, if suitably calculated, turns out to be highly beneficial.

When running uphill and during (speed-)hiking, a new component enters the calculation, namely gravitational Power P_g (see previous Section 2.1). It depends linearly both on the runner's weight and the vertical speed and can be accurately calculated if this data is properly known. Figure 2.3 shows both the gravitational and the total Power as a function of inclination/vertical speed and a fixed running velocity of 8 km/h. Apart from small slopes, P_g plays a significant role and even dominates over the other Power com-

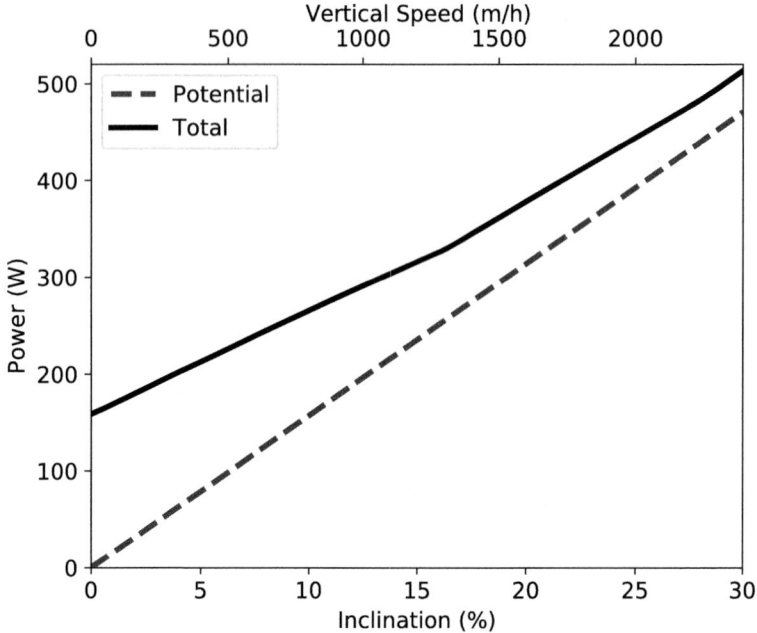

Figure 2.3: Evolution of potential (gravitational) and total Power as a function of inclination and vertical speed for a runner with 72 kg and a fixed running speed of 8 km/h.

ponents for steeper ascents, which certainly matches your experience. However, what's noteworthy is that while the remaining parts still play a role, their contribution decreases for larger inclinations despite the constant velocity. In other words, just summing up all the different parts doesn't lead to the correct solution in this case. The reason is that with increasing inclination, more and more "other" Power is directly converted into gravitational energy. For instance, think about vertical Power: As we have seen, the jump performed during each stride constitutes an essential part of Power for flat running, where the entire body is lifted and then descends again by several centimeters. When running up a mountain, you still lift your body during each stride, but it doesn't go down the entire distance anymore. This means that part of the vertical Power was used for gravitational energy.

The fact that for steeper slopes running/speed-hiking Power mainly consists of the gravitational component means that this is a very effective way of movement. The immense advantage of cyclists on flat terrain completely vanishes for gradients of 15% or larger. Climbing up a mountain with a desired vertical velocity requires a specific amount of gravitational Power, which solely depends on the weight that needs to be lifted, irrespective of the type of movement. It is physically impossible to climb at that vertical speed with a Power lower than that. Since a cyclist needs to lift their own weight plus the one of their bicycle, steep inclines are thus even easier by foot.

Ideally, your Power meter takes arbitrary inclinations properly into account and works equally well for both running and walking, where the latter is more efficient for larger slopes when the speed gets lower. Higher efficiency means that you need less Power to climb at a given vertical pace or can alternatively go faster with the same amount of Power. For those of you that are well-trained in both speed hiking and flat running, there shouldn't be much difference between the Power that you can exert for these types of motion. Your muscles are then adapted adequately to both, whereas there might be a disagreement for those whose training is inclined in one direction. Regardless of which type you belong to, you should find out how your Power meter reacts when switching between the two. I have already seen statements from manufacturers saying that the higher efficiency of speed hiking naturally implies a lower Power output, which is why the goals have to be set lower for their product in this case. You might notice that this contradicts the remarks above, which brings us back to the previous considerations that there is not one exact way of calculating Power but different opinions and methods to do so. It's certainly an advantage if you don't have to differentiate between various conditions and adapt your goal Power accordingly. But in case that is necessary for your choice of Power meter, you just need to find out how it behaves.

2.5 DOWNHILL

Once you've reached the end of an ascent and enter the downhill phase, vertical speed and gravitation go in the same direction. Whereas during a climb you have to work against the gravitational force and exert corresponding Power, when running downhill the gravitational field of the Earth exerts Power *on you*. For slight downhills with gradients down to around -10%, this additional Power comes in quite handy. Whereas during flat and uphill running, you have to lift your body actively, the vertical oscillation necessary to maintain the running motion is for such slight to medium descents increasingly provided by gravitational energy. Therefore, less Power has to be provided by the body, making it easier to run at a certain speed. For downhills steeper than -10%, the situation changes again: Now the gravitational force gets so large that you have to actively work against it. The biophysical processes of running are complex, and just because Power is now externally provided does not mean that they can arbitrarily be sped up. On a bicycle, you naturally switch to freewheeling in that case, but just imagine your bicycle wouldn't have that possibility. You'd end up with the same problem like with running sooner or later. So, all in all, for steeper downhills your muscles have to work against the further acceleration of your body. This running type also requires Power, but it is typically lower than running flat or uphill, which is important for trail runners who want to use Power as a metric for training and racing. Trying to run at a prescribed Power on even or positively inclined terrain is one thing; trying to do so downhill can be dangerous. The impact on the body under these conditions should not be underestimated, so don't try to run faster than you're used to just to reach a Power goal.

2.6 TRAIL RUNNING

If you occasionally run on technical terrain, you certainly agree that constantly adapting to an uneven surface requires additional effort and thus Power. For trail runners, a proper characterization of this supplementary component is crucial but not at all easy to determine, requiring a reliable source with instant information. Even with that, a calibration of the applied algorithm is everything but easy. In principle, technical sections lead to an ever-changing running style, where the level of inhomogeneity reflects how technical the part appears to the runner. Measured quantities that are sensitive to this can thus be used to estimate the corresponding trail Power, which is illustrated in Figure 2.4. It shows vertical oscillation and cadence during part of a run which includes the transition from a non-technical forest road to a medium-technical trail. Both metrics are almost constant on the non-technical section, but with the start of the technical trail, they react just like a seismograph needle deflects during an earthquake. This makes it possible to quantify the trail Power by continuously analyzing the *variation* of such variables.

It is worth mentioning that if you'd let two runners with the same bodyweight run the same path at the same speed, the resulting trail Power will likely not be the same. If one of them is more experienced in running technical trails, they will probably master the section more fluently, i.e., with a

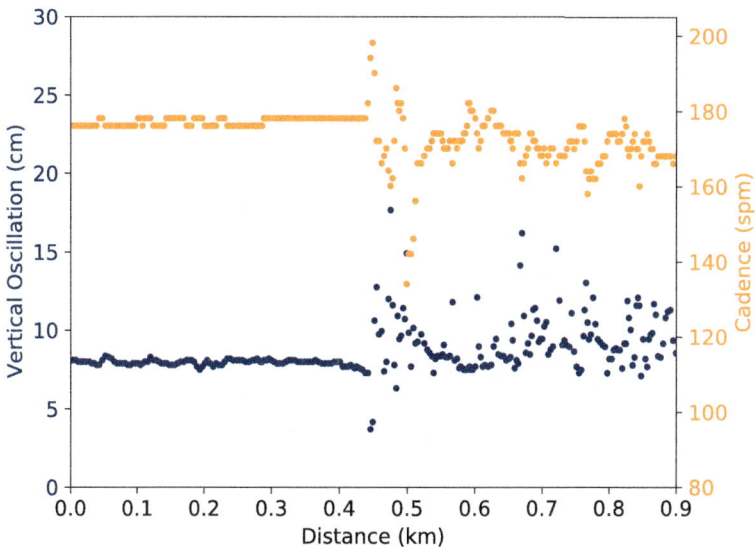

Figure 2.4: Measured values of vertical oscillation and cadence on a non-technical forest road (left part) with an abrupt transition to a medium-technical trail.

more homogeneous running style and thus a lower trail Power.

2.7 CONCLUDING OVERVIEW

As we have seen, many parameters have to be considered for calculating one number corresponding to a runner's exerted Power. Before we jump to Power-based training, let us take a concluding look at some exemplary situations, all of them illustrated in Figure 2.5 and again using the same Power-calculation model as before.

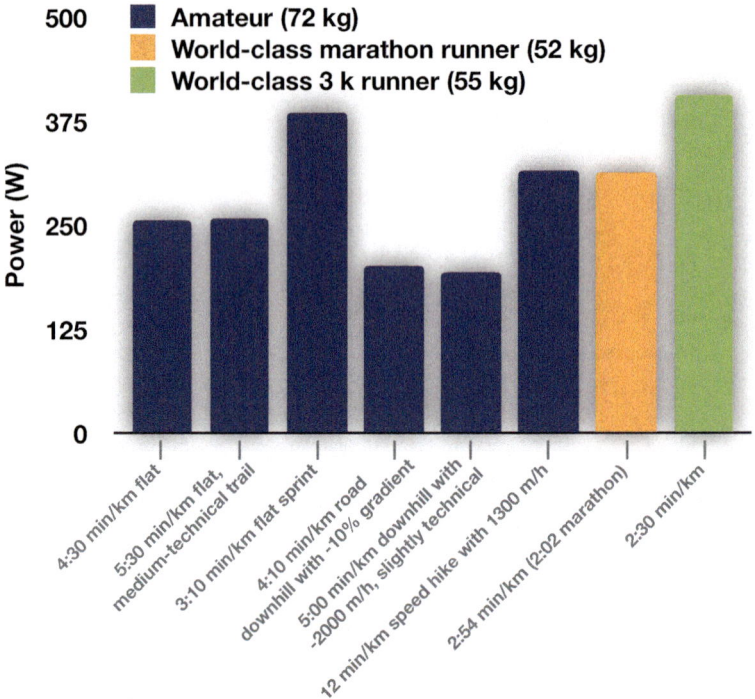

Figure 2.5: Total exerted Power for different running conditions.

The first example is our reference runner with a bodyweight of 72 kg and a height of 184 cm, running on a flat road at a 4:30 min/km pace. In this case, the Power output is 255 W, corresponding to the sum of individual components as displayed in Figure 2.2 at around 13.3 km/h. Just as discussed before, the final number depends not only on the runner's weight, height, and speed, but also their cadence and vertical oscillation as well as the wind speed. When switching from the road to a medium-technical trail, holding the same Power corresponds to a slower pace because of the additional trail component. Of course, increasing the Power output allows for a faster pace both on technical and non-technical terrain. For downhill running at small to medium inclinations, the gravitational force helps to run faster, allowing the reference runner to maintain 4:10 min/km at -10% gradient with comparatively low 201 W. Even steeper slopes again remove part of this advantage through the additional muscular load to work against gravitation. All the energy released downhill naturally doesn't come for free but has to be earned uphill. Because of gravitational Power, a speed hike with a relatively slow pace of only 12 min/km costs more than 310 W if an altitude gain of 1300 m per hour is accomplished. That, in turn, corresponds to the Power output of a world-class marathon runner during his world-record attempt. Maybe you start to wonder that something must be wrong here because you assume that an amateur could never keep the Power output of such an outstanding professional for longer than a few seconds or minutes. So, where's the catch? It's the weight: The excellent marathon runner discussed here weighs only 52 kg and thus 20 kg less than the amateur. Presuming that part of this difference comes from additional muscles, a comparable Power level is achievable even for well-trained non-professionals. However, the weight difference directly implies a slower pace for the heavier runner.

3 - IMPORTANT METRICS

With the previous chapter in mind, you now know what is relevant to calculate a runner's Power. However, to properly utilize the resulting number for training and racing, there are a few related quantities which need to be introduced. Many of them are by now standard in the field and were initially adapted from cycling, where Power-based training is ahead by several years. In contrast, other quantities are newly introduced here specifically for trail and ultra runners. Throughout this chapter, we will use data from a particular runner with a bodyweight of 72 kg as an example to illustrate all of them.

3.1 FUNCTIONAL THRESHOLD POWER

Before introducing all the different quantities to analyze a given workout or race, one fundamental metric needs to be defined first: The Functional Threshold Power, abbreviated to FTP. A runner's FTP is often called rFTP to separate it from its cycling counterpart, but here we'll just use the term FTP and assume that the correct respective value is used for each sport.

The concept of the FTP was introduced by Andrew Coggan, Ph.D., to classify the measured Power numbers of an athlete (see reference 2). It corresponds to the maximum

Power that can be maintained for the duration of one hour. Since such a maximum effort for that duration would be counterproductive and not even feasible as part of a training session, the FTP is typically estimated using shorter tests of around 20 minutes length. It is the Power equivalent of your threshold pace, which you might be familiar with. For most runners, it lies between their 10 k and their half-marathon race paces. If you know your threshold pace, choose a flat course on a calm day, warm up for 10 minutes and then run at that pace as constantly as possible for around 6-10 minutes (or longer if you like). Your FTP then simply corresponds to the average Power yielded during this threshold interval.

If you do not know your threshold pace, you determine it from a tempo training run. After a proper warm-up phase of around 10 minutes, the general goal of this test is to run as uniformly but also fast as possible for 20 minutes. The FTP is then estimated as follows:

- Calculate the average Power of the tempo part of the run, but exclude the first five minutes.
- Divide the resulting number by 1.02. This correction accounts for the fact that even during training, you can run with a slightly higher Power than your FTP.

This FTP test is illustrated in Figure 3.1. The average Power amounts to 339 W in this case, excluding the first five minutes of the tempo section. The estimated FTP value is then 339 W / 1.02 = 332 W.

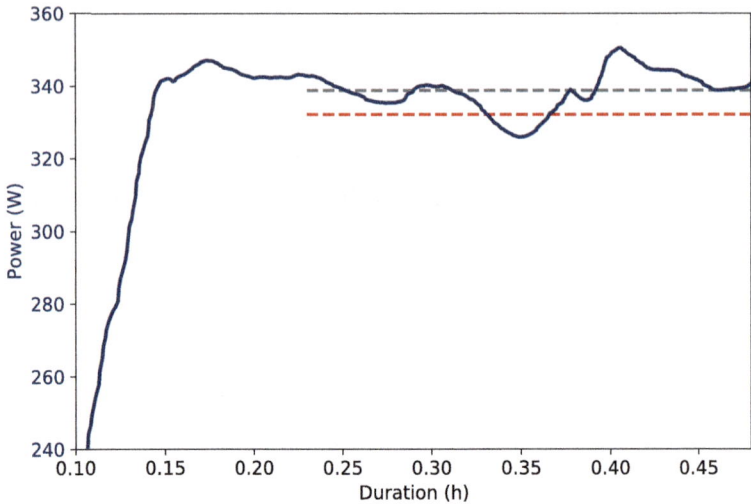

Figure 3.1: Power chart of a threshold run. The average Power of the FTP evaluation part is shown with a dashed grey line. Correspondingly, the derived FTP of 332 W is drawn in red.

As already mentioned, the values of your running and speed-hiking FTPs might differ, depending on your training focus and Power meter. If you suspect that your Power meter reacts differently to flat than uphill terrain, think about carrying out one FTP test for each (but not on consecutive days). The two values can afterwards be averaged, depending on your training and racing focus.

3.2 POWER ZONES

With a properly determined FTP, it is common practice in Power-based training to divide the different Power levels into training zones. This helps to put the obtained numbers into perspective, where the zones are typically defined as ranges in percent of the FTP. That way, it is possible to have generic Power zones which apply to different runners or the same runner when the FTP changes. Such a categorization is very useful for defining workouts and setting a proper training focus, but there are a few caveats that should be kept in mind:

- In reality, there is no hard transition between the different zones. Furthermore, the intensity range covered within one zone is generally quite extensive. Try to think of these zones more as general guidance, putting rough labels on the different Power numbers.

- Different Power meters generally use independent algorithms for calculating a runner's Power. This naturally leads to inconsistent results, not only in terms of absolute but also of relative Power. For example, let's say we'd let a runner wear two different Power meters during the same activity, first running at threshold pace and then more relaxed. After the considerations in the previous chapter, we shouldn't be surprised to see diverging results for the Power calculated at threshold pace, i.e., the FTP. It is, however, also possible that during the following relaxed stage one of the Power meters displays a

Power that corresponds to 70% of the respective FTP, whereas for the other one it deviates by a few percent.

- Although a given definition may suggest otherwise, Power zones are certainly not carved in stone. There are different definitions and opinions behind them, and the applicability of a specific one primarily depends on the training focus.

The last point is especially important in the context of this book since the Power-zone definition used here considerably differs from the one currently widely used in Power-based running, which was introduced by Jim Vance (see references 3 and 4). According to that definition, the first zone, labelled "Walking/Recovery", covers everything below 81% of an athlete's FTP. Such a definition might make sense for those who train and race not longer than for three hours, such as half-marathon or even fast marathon runners. However, if you are preparing for a trail marathon or an ultra race, then you would, if you train correctly, spend a large fraction of your training (and maybe even racing) in this "recovery" zone. I guess you'd agree that 70-80% FTP feels like everything else but recovery after four, ten, let alone 20 hours or more.

Instead, I prefer to use the Power zones introduced by Andrew Coggan (Ph.D.) for cyclists (reference 5) also for running. Despite the differences between the two sports, these zones are generally also well suited for trail and ultra runners. An overview of them is given in Table 3.1, showing

Zone	Focus	Power (% of FTP)	Power for example runner with FTP = 332 W
1	Active Recovery	< 55	< 183 W
2	Endurance	55 - 75	184 - 249 W
3	Tempo	76 - 90	250 - 299 W
4	Lactate Threshold	91 - 105	300 - 349 W
5	VO_2 Max	106 - 120	350 - 398 W
6	Anaerobic Capacity	121 - 150	399 - 498 W
7	Neuromuscular Power	> 150	> 499 W

Table 3.1: Power zones for long- and ultra-distance runners, applying the definition from Andrew Coggan (Ph.D.) for cyclists.

the corresponding Power ranges both in percent of the FTP and also in watts for our example runner with an FTP of 332 W (see the previous section). The focus column puts a rough label on each zone. Let's quickly discuss running-related applications and typical situations for the seven different zones. If you are interested in a more detailed and generic explanation, please have a look at reference 5.

- **1 / Active Recovery:** On flat terrain, this zone covers walking and (for faster runners) also very relaxed running and is mainly reserved for interval recovery. However, on trails and in the mountains, it might also be reached for some downhills or very technical sections.

- **2 / Endurance:** This relaxed zone should be the focus of ultra races longer than ten hours as well as long training runs. It can also be used for moderate interval recovery.

- **3 / Tempo:** It is the primary zone for races between three and ten hours and can also be used to set training stimuli during both shorter and longer runs. The wide duration range indicates that it makes quite some difference if you're near the lower or the upper bound.

- **4 / Lactate Threshold:** This zone is mainly used for faster tempo (i.e., threshold) runs to build endurance at higher intensities. It is vital for those targeting shorter races or when trying to improve speed basis, such as in the off-season.

- **5 / VO$_2$ Max:** Often used for medium intervals of up to around five minutes (see, for example, the workouts "8 x 3 min" and "1 min / 1 min" in Section 6.1). Training in this zone is also very efficient for long-distance runners.

- **6 / Anaerobic Capacity:** This zone is used for intervals of short duration, which can also be part of the off-season training to improve the general speed.

- **7 / Neuromuscular Power:** The effort in this zone can only be held for a very short amount of time (typically less than 30 s). Such short sprints can be helpful to put a new stimulus to the muscles.

3.3 WORKOUT METRICS

There are several derived quantities that can be calculated after finishing a workout or a race with a running Power meter. Some of them should be automatically calculated and displayed by the training platform you use to display and analyze the workout. The quantities are discussed using the example of a training run whose Power chart and altitude profile are shown in Figure 3.2. It corresponds to a mountain trail run of a runner with an FTP of 332 W.

Average Power

The average Power (AP) is the most basic of all workout metrics, obtained by averaging the runner's Power output over time. For the example run in Figure 3.2, AP amounts to 246 W and is illustrated with a dotted line. You can see how it nicely marks the middle of the Power profile, which comes by definition, but only when the Power is plotted over time instead of distance. As ancillary information, one horsepower is defined as 745.7 W, so $AP \approx 1/3\,hp$ in this case. That may help put the Power numbers into perspective, but as you likely have expected, you don't stand a chance against your car.

Normalized Power

In general, our body performs most efficiently when the effort is distributed constantly over a workout. Variation leads to additional fatigue, which is not taken into account

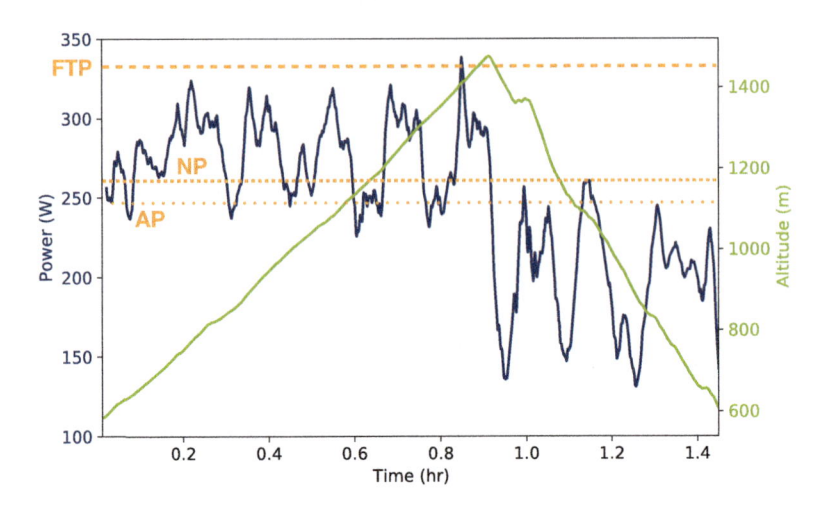

Figure 3.2: Power chart and altitude profile of an example training run, including the runner's FTP as well as normalized and average Power of the run.

by the calculation of the average Power. You've probably already (maybe subconsciously) noticed this when realizing that your average pace after an interval run on flat terrain is considerably slower than that of others at constant speeds that were similarly or even less exhausting. This is where the normalized Power (NP) comes in, which was introduced by the training platform *Training Peaks* (see reference 6). The exact formula is more complex to write up, so we are just discussing it schematically here. For the calculation of the NP, the values in the Power chart are smoothed using a time window of 30 seconds to average out small-scale fluctuations. Then the level of variation of the resulting profile is quantified. If the Power output of the session was constant, then the normalized Power is equal to the average Power. The larger the variation of the profile is, the higher the resulting NP becomes. It is defined such that its result estimates the average Power of a run with constant effort and the same physiological intensity.

Let's take the workout in Figure 3.2 as an example: During the ascent, the Power was varied between around 250 W and 300 W every few minutes, and for the descent it was generally lower. Sections with 300 W tire the body more than it can recover at 200 W while descending, so the AP of 246 W underestimates the physiological load. The normalized Power is, in this case, 260 W, which should correspond to a better estimate of the effective intensity of this trail run.

Variability Index

As the name suggests, the variability index (VI) quantifies the level of variability of a workout. The normalized Power already takes fluctuations into account, but without any reference its pure value does not reveal how the effort was performed. However, this is not a problem as we already know what to use as a reference value, namely the average Power. The variability index is therefore simply defined as

$$VI = \frac{NP}{AP}.$$

For our example run, $VI = 260\,W/246\,W = 1.057$. In case of a constant effort, the variability index stays close to 1.00, whereas it can reach values of 1.20 or higher for runs with many short intervals.

Intensity Factor

Both average and normalized Power are very helpful quantities, but they are strongly tied to a runner's weight and height, running style, and performance. Comparing the Power output of two different runners is therefore of limited use, even if they use the same Power meter. Furthermore, seeing how your own running Power evolves can be pretty motivating, but for evaluating workouts and defining the Power aim for a race, we need something more general.

For that reason, Andrew Coggan, PhD, developed the intensity factor (IF, see also reference 7), which can be calculated as follows:

$$\text{IF} = \frac{\text{NP}}{\text{FTP}}.$$

It is a straightforward calculation, but just dividing the normalized Power by the FTP greatly helps to put it into perspective. For the run in Figure 3.2, we get IF = 260 W/332 W = 0.78, which corresponds to medium intensity relative to the runner's capabilities.

Time-Corrected Intensity Factor

By relating the normalized Power to the FTP, the intensity factor properly characterizes the intensity of a run. While it is commonly used for that purpose, the characteristic that the relative intensity is always given with respect to the

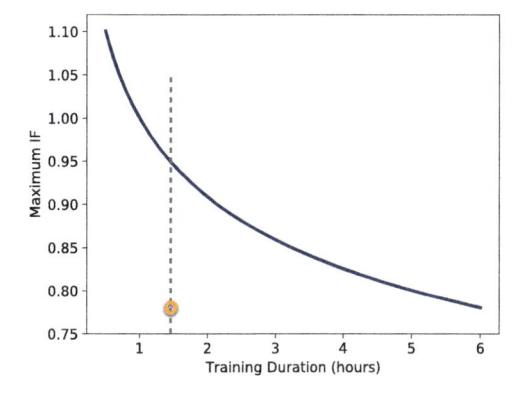

Training Duration	Maximum IF
30 min	1.10
1 h	1.00
1.5 h	0.95
2 h	0.91
2.5 h	0.88
3 h	0.86
4 h	0.83
5 h	0.80
6 h	0.78

Figure 3.3: Maximum intensity factor as a function of training duration (left). The orange circle corresponds to the example run from Figure 3.2. The table on the right gives the values of IF_{max} for different specific durations.

one-hour maximum Power (i.e., the FTP) is certainly not ideal for all use cases. Because of fatigue, the maximum achievable intensity IF_{max} is strongly time-dependent. Especially when planning and evaluating longer training runs, this has to be taken into account.

The estimated IF_{max} is given as a function of training duration in Figure 3.3. Please note that these values are to be used for subsequent calculations and reference and should thus generally not be reached in your training. Otherwise, you would turn your training runs into races, which would neither be healthy nor even effective.

Using IF_{max} for the given training duration, we can define the time-corrected intensity factor as

$$\text{TIF} = \frac{\text{IF}}{\text{IF}_{max}}.$$

As for our example, the workout duration was almost 1 1/2 hours, yielding $\text{IF}_{max} \approx 0.95$ according to the table in Figure 3.3. The time-corrected intensity factor is thus TIF = 0.78/0.95 = 0.82, denoting the fraction of applied Power in relation to the runner's achievable maximum for this duration.

For those who want to calculate IF_{max} for arbitrary durations, the values given in Figure 3.3 are the result of the following function:

$$\text{IF}_{max}(t) = t^{-0.1383},$$

where t is the workout duration in units of hours. It has to be noted that this exact relation is not really carved in stone and varies a bit from runner to runner. Nevertheless, it should generally be well applicable to trained endurance athletes. What also needs to be mentioned is that, to my knowledge, the TIF is introduced here for the first time. It is therefore currently not yet implemented in any training platform. However, if the one you use allows adding custom calculations or in case you manually keep records of your training (for example, with a spreadsheet as described in Section 4.2), just try adding the TIF for further insight into your workout sessions. We will further discuss how to make use of the TIF in Chapters 4 and 5.

Training Stress Score

Both the IF and the TIF are defined to characterize the intensity of a training session, but what we still need is a variable that quantifies the total physiological stress. Surely a quick 20-minute run has a lower impact on the body than a long run with a duration of several hours, even if the TIF is identical for both. To estimate the physiological load, Andrew Coggan (Ph.D.) introduced the Training Stress Score (TSS) alongside NP and IF (see again reference 7). Unfortunately, many references (both other literature and on the internet) use an unnecessarily confusing combination of NP, IF, FTP, and workout duration for the definition of the TSS, making it harder to understand what's behind it. Here is the straightforward formula of the TSS:

$$\text{TSS} = \text{IF}^2 \cdot t \cdot 100,$$

where t again denotes the workout duration in hours. According to the definition, the TSS depends quadratically on IF and linearly on t. Let's discuss a few examples to get familiar with the formula:

1. A race with a duration of 1 hour, i.e., $t = 1.00$. If the FTP was adequately set and the runner was performing at maximum, $\text{IF} = 1.00$. The square of 1.00 is again 1.00, so the TSS amounts to $\text{TSS} = 1.00 \cdot 1 \cdot 100 = \underline{100}$ in this case.

2. A training run with $t = 1$ and $\text{IF} = 0.8$. Here we get $\text{TSS} = 0.8 \cdot 0.8 \cdot 1 \cdot 100 = 0.64 \cdot 100 = \underline{64}$. The qua-

dratic dependency on the IF incorporates that moving at a given percentage of the FTP has a disproportional influence on the physiological load.

3. A long run with a duration of 3 h 45 min and IF = 0.7. Here we have to first convert the duration into a floating-point number: $t = 3 + \frac{45 \min}{60 \min} = 3.75$. The TSS is then TSS = $0.7 \cdot 0.7 \cdot 3.75 \cdot 100 = \underline{183.75}$. Despite the moderate intensity, you'll likely feel the larger physiological impact of long runs on your body, confirming that the calculation of the TSS is indeed reasonable.

4. For the sake of completeness, the example run of this section exhibits TSS = 90.2.

The TSS is a handy tool to monitor an athlete's physiological load over time and even plan future workouts to maximize training success and avoid overtraining.

Exerted Work and Energy Consumption

In case you already train with a Power meter, perhaps you have noticed something in the workout summary on your training platform called "Total exerted work" or just "Total work". It denotes the overall physical work exerted during a workout, which is calculated easiest by multiplying the average Power and the duration:

$W_{tot} = AP \cdot t$.

It is typically displayed in units of kilojoule (kJ). For our example run, the calculation to end up in this unit is

$$W_{tot} = \frac{246}{1000} \text{ kW} \cdot (1 \cdot 3600 + 28 \cdot 60) \text{ s} = 0.246 \text{ kW} \cdot 5280 \text{ s} = \underline{1299 \text{ kJ}}.$$

Here we converted the AP to units of kilowatts and multiplied it with the workout duration of 1 h 28 min in seconds, which directly gives the total work in units of kilojoule.

W_{tot} is a fundamental physical quantity and belongs to the standard output in most workout summaries. Still, its direct usefulness for training evaluation and planning is rather low. It can, however, be used to estimate the total energy consumption of the body in units of (kilo)calories. Only a certain fraction of the metabolic energy is converted into external energy/Power. This efficiency is hard to determine, and it has to be assumed that it varies over time and depends on the runner as well as on how the external Power is calculated. Despite all these inaccuracies, it has to be kept in mind that the alternative way of estimating the amount of burned calories, namely via the measured heart rate, is also everything else but accurate. The Power-based calculation thus provides an independent estimate which might even be more precise in some cases, such as, e.g., longer runs. In the case of this section's example run, the Power-based assessment gives 1244 kcal, whereas the one using the heart rate yields 1182 kcal. In this case, the heart-rate data was measured with a respective belt, providing very accurate values. Wrist-based measurements are still often inaccurate, leading to a corresponding uncertainty of all derived values, including the energy consumption.

Trail Score

As seen in the previous chapter, the additional effort of technical sections can be quantified by a Power meter. If done so, this leads to a better estimate of the exerted Power, greatly extending the range of terrain for which it is usable. Furthermore, the estimated trail Power can be compared to the overall one, thus quantifying how technical a trail was for the runner. This trail score (TSC) is again a new concept; I can't recall coming across it before. In case the Power meter can calculate the trail Power P_{tr} independently from the total one P_{tot}, its calculation is pretty straightforward:

$$\text{TSC} = \frac{P_{tr}}{P_{tot}} \cdot 100,$$

with the factor 100 applied to convert the value into percent. The trail score thus measures the ratio of the trail to the total Power.

This is illustrated for our example mountain run in Figure 3.4, where several sections are highlighted to ease the discussion. During the uphill part, the values are generally relatively low, rarely exceeding 10%. The reason for that is the gravitational Power which makes up a significant fraction of P_{tot}. Nevertheless, differences are visible: Sections (1) and (3) correspond to partly narrow hiking paths with many roots and rocks. On the other hand, Section (2) was a gravel forest road, allowing smooth and efficient running with an almost negligible trail score. During the downhill part, (4) and (6) stand out with their comparably large TSC of around 20-30%. The trail of (6) was notably the same as

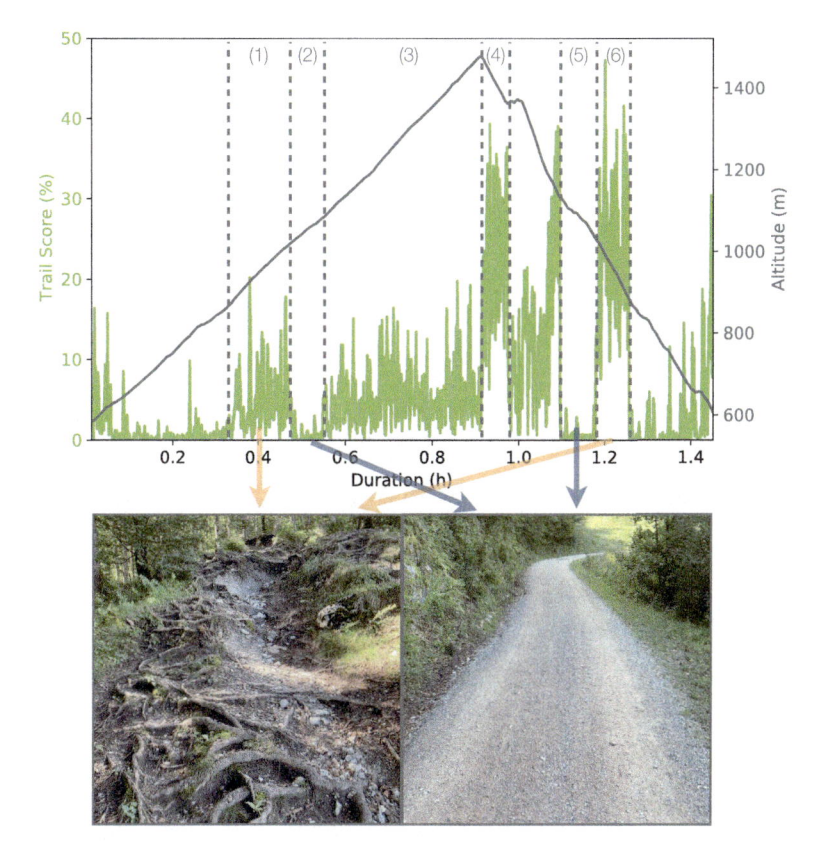

Figure 3.4: Trail score as a function of time for the example run. Sections (1) and (6) correspond to the same trail, and the forest road of (2) is contained in (5). Pictures of the two paths are added for illustration.

that of (1), but running it downhill naturally requires a lot of technical effort. In contrast, the values are close to 0 during (5), appropriately reflecting the smooth running style that was possible on the corresponding gravel road. The average TSC for this run was 5.8%. This value alone is a bit lost without comparison, but it can be put into perspective in combination with the ones of other runs.

The quantification of technical effort via the TSC can serve as a general measure to classify routes for trail runners, both for training and races. Similar to the difficulty grades of climbing, training platforms and race organizers could evaluate the TSC of individual sections or routes (ideally by averaging the data of several people who ran them) and provide the information to the runners. This would allow them to prepare themselves better or leave out a section/race in case they consider it too technical.

Grade-Adjusted Pace

For road runners that primarily train and race on flat terrain, pace is probably the most decisive of all metrics. As however already discussed in the previous chapter, the situation is entirely different for trail runners. Though the overall pace can certainly be used to, e.g., evaluate a runner's performance over time for a given course, it makes no sense to compare paces obtained on different tracks due to the generally largely different conditions. To overcome these limitations, the grade-adjusted pace (GAP) was introduced by the training platform strava (see references 8 and 9), based on a publication by Minetti et al. (reference 10), and further improved using data from strava users. Similar to the considerations regarding Power in this book, the idea behind the GAP is to correct the actual pace for the slope to estimate with which pace the athlete would run with the same effort on flat terrain. This allows comparing runs with different amounts of ascents and descents, including flat runs. The advantage of the grade-adjusted pace lies in its simplicity: While the underlying model corresponds to a simplification and is not equally valid for all runners, the GAP is calculated by just using the pace and the gradient. Technical/trail effort is not taken into account, so the resulting GAP is generally too slow for trail runs. The average GAP of the example run is 4:58 min/km, which is a conservative estimate of the pace of a run with a similar effort on flat terrain because of the technical sections.

Equivalent Flat Pace

With the more precise and user-specific data recorded by a Power meter, it is possible to estimate better what the runner's corresponding pace on a flat road with the same Power output would be. Just as the TIF and the TSC, this equivalent flat pace (EFP) is, as far as I know, newly introduced here and thus not yet implemented in any training platform.

The idea behind the EFP is to check at which pace on a flat road the runner would move with the same Power output as the measured one, where the algorithm uses the athlete-specific functional relation that is shown in Figure 2.2 (Power vs. velocity on flat terrain). Here both the average as well as the normalized Power can be used, depending on the interest. For the example trail run, EFP_{AP} = 4:40 min/km, notably faster than the corresponding GAP. EFP_{NP} is even faster, estimated at 4:25 min/km. One reason for the discrepancy between GAP and EFP$_{AP}$ is the consideration of the technical effort for the Power calculation. Therefore, the EFP should provide a better estimate of the equivalent pace on flat terrain. In addition to that, the run was carried out with a small backpack whose weight was considered for the Power calculation, whereas only the user's weight entered the calculation of the EFP, making the result better comparable to a flat run without additional weight. In case the relation of Power vs. flat-running speed is unknown, the algorithm can still estimate the EFP using average cadence and vertical oscillation of the same run, but with reduced accuracy.

Running Efficiency

If your running Power meter separately measures the component related to the vertical oscillation (see section "Flat Running" in the previous chapter), it can estimate your running efficiency for flat sections. One way to do so is by dividing the vertical Power (sometimes also called "form Power") by the total Power and converting the obtained ratio to percent, which we'll call the run score (RSC) here:

$$\text{RSC} = \frac{P_{\text{ver}}}{P_{\text{tot}}} \cdot 100.$$

As already discussed, the vertical component that is related to P_{ver} is necessary to sustain the running motion but doesn't directly contribute to the forward motion. The goal of every runner should thus be to minimize the RSC as much as possible, keeping in mind that comparisons of this

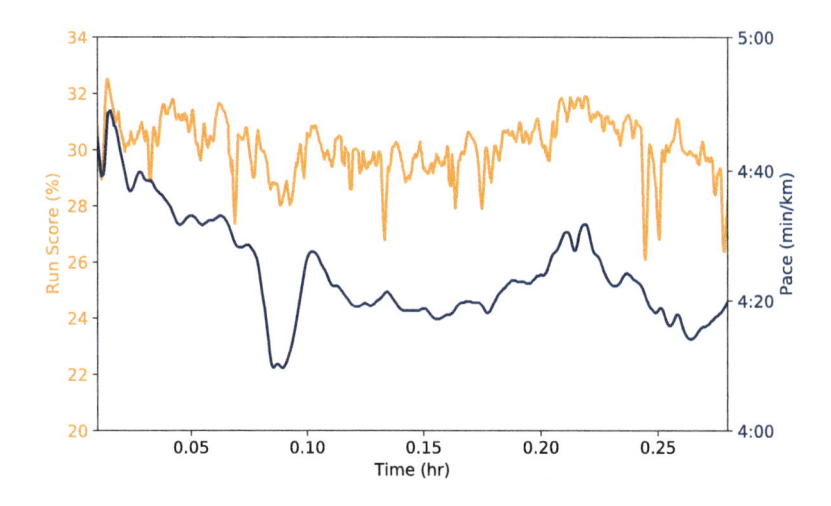

Figure 3.5: Graph of the RSC for a flat section of a training run, shown together with the pace.

value are only meaningful for a fixed pace as well as flat sections. Given the different composition of P_{tot} for ascents and descents, a proper evaluation of the running efficiency is not straightforward in this case though generally possible when separating sections of different slopes and excluding those with technical effort. Instead of using the same example run as before, the evolution of the RSC is shown for a flat section in Figure 3.5, together with the pace. Estimates of the running efficiency depend considerably on the used Power meter and should therefore only be compared when using the same device.

4 - TRAINING FOUNDATION

The different metrics that were introduced in the previous chapter are valuable tools to analyze your running workouts. Keeping them in mind, we will now focus on how to efficiently integrate a running Power meter into a training routine, including an evaluation of the short- and long-term training load.

4.1 POWER AND HEART RATE

Contrary to cycling, Power-based training for runners is essentially still in its infancy. As of today, most athletes still mostly base their training on their heart rates and paces. This directly brings us to the following questions:

1. What are the benefits of using Power for training as compared to the heart rate?

To answer this question, let us first differentiate Power and heart rate in terms of what they measure. After having read the previous chapters (and maybe even before), you already know quite a bit about running Power. It is a physical quantity that describes an athlete's mechanical effort (work) per time. Just like the pace, Power is an *external* metric. This means that while it results from a myriad of processes inside the body, it can (and has to) be determined

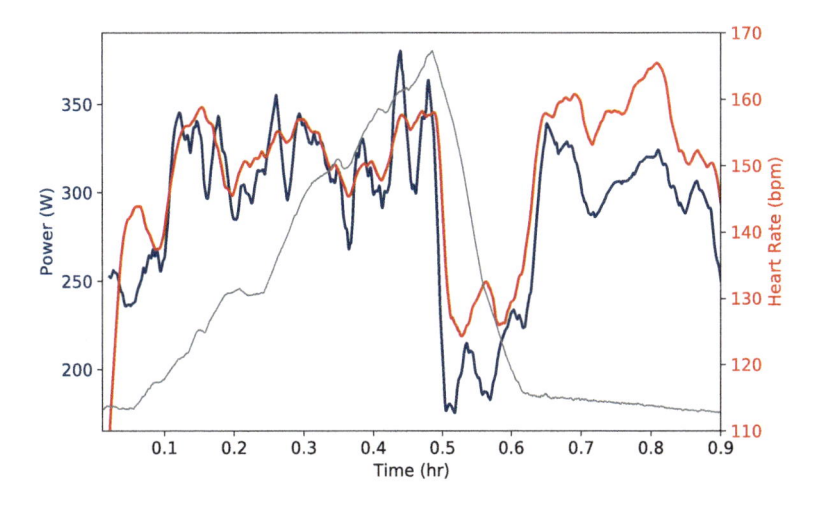

Figure 4.1: Progression of Power and heart rate for a high-intensity training near a runner's FTP. The altitude profile is indicated with a thin grey line, showing that the dip at the beginning of the second half relates to a downhill section.

entirely from external variables. In contrast, heart rate is an *internal* biological quantity. It reacts to different variables, where the metabolic effort and, correspondingly, the exerted Power is surely the most important one. The strong correlation between Power and heart rate is nicely visible in Figure 4.1, showing both for a workout with high intensity, again using data of the same example runner as before. Almost every rise of the calculated Power is followed by an increase of the recorded heart rate, typically with a slight delay. This reaction time of our heart, which is usually at the order of 30-60 seconds, is often quoted as one of the main advantages of using a Power meter - of course by those who like to convince you that you should buy one - instead of the measured heart rate. Personally, I consider this delay as less important in most situations. Although it is indeed nice for, e.g., better pacing of intervals, this effect alone would likely not justify purchasing a Power meter for most runners. So what else does justify it then? As already said before, the metabolic effort is the most important influence on the heart rate, but it is not the only one. Let's again look at Figure 4.1, now a bit more thoroughly. The run basically consisted of two separate parts with similarly high intensity, separated by a downhill section at lower effort, which served as recovery. An identical Power goal had been defined for the two sections in advance, alternately targeting ~ 325 W and 300 W, switching every kilometer. When comparing Power and heart rate for the two parts, there is indeed an obvious correlation within each, but the heart rate is generally higher during the second one. This effect, which is well visible by the fact that both graphs are not overlapping anymore, is usually called cardiac drift. Influences such as dehydration and fatigue cause our heart to beat harder over time to maintain a given Power output. While this explanation sounds simple, the extent of the cardiac drift depends on many influences and is thus generally unknown during the training. Now try to imagine how this workout would have looked if it was based on the heart rate, ignoring the data from the Power meter. For properly defined heart-rate goals, the first high-intensity section would likely have looked very similar. However, aiming for the same heart-rate

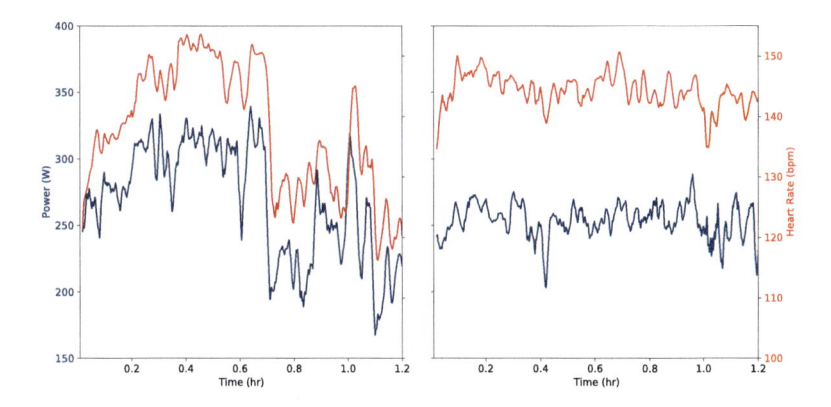

Figure 4.2: Power and heart rate graphs for two runs of the same athlete and with identical y-axis scaling. The training on the left was performed under normal conditions, the one on the right during hot and humid weather.

zones during the second part means that the resulting Power would have been considerably lower, which would have made this training less effective than it was with the usage of the Power-meter data.

Apart from parameters that influence an athlete's heart rate during a run, it is affected by internal and external factors, which can generally shift it up or down. Internal factors include:

- Sleep duration and quality.
- Stress level.
- Alcohol and caffeine consumption.
- Residual exhaustion from past workouts.

Crucial external factors are air temperature and humidity. Their impact can be severe, as is illustrated in Figure 4.2, showing both Power and heart rate for two runs that happened roughly three weeks apart but under vastly different conditions. The one on the left side took place under normal conditions, the one on the right on a hot and humid day. Such weather puts additional stress on the body, leading to an elevated heart rate. This impact is clearly visible when comparing the two examples. As for the "normal" run, the heart rate only slightly surpasses 150 bpm during the section with around 300 W Power and quickly drops to about 130 bpm afterwards. Regarding the "heat" run, the heart rate lies between 140 bpm and 150 bpm despite the comparably moderate, constant Power level of 250 W. If the goal of this run had been defined on the heart rate, a much lower Power output and corresponding muscular load would have been the result. All this perhaps sounds as if Power meters should completely replace heart-rate monitoring, which brings us to the next question.

2. Should heart-rate data be ignored when running with a Power meter?

The quick and definite answer is: No! Despite the enormous advancements of running-Power meters within the last years, the frequency with which our heart beats still delivers highly valuable information. Given that exerted Power is an external and heart rate an internal quantity, the latter should rather be seen as providing complementary information. Regular heart-rate monitoring, both during workouts and in general, is an important puzzle piece for your training. To obtain accurate heart-rate data, I generally recommend wearing a chest strap instead of relying on your sports watch's optical heart-rate (OHR) sensor during a workout. Despite advancements of the latter in recent years, they are mostly still far from accurate. However, if you are satisfied with the OHR measurement of your watch or don't feel comfortable wearing a strap, you just have to be aware of the reduced accuracy.

The following hypothetical situations illustrate how to make use of heart-rate data:

- You have a specific workout planned, but unfortunately, the weather turns out to be extremely hot. It should be obvious to avoid the greatest heat of the day and try to run in the morning or the evening, but you still want to follow your schedule. Blindly following a specific goal can be inefficient for your training and, in the worst case, even dangerous to your health, depending on the exact conditions, your constitution, and your target intensity. If you are still fully convinced that the planned training is feasible, you could proceed as follows: You begin with the workout as planned, continuously monitor your heart rate, and (even more important) check how you feel. If you already feel that it is not a good idea right from the beginning, you should lower the goal or skip the training altogether. If that's not the case, you can continue. As we have seen before, an increased heart rate is not unusual and even expected under such circumstances. The trick is now to distinguish an acceptable deviation from an unac-

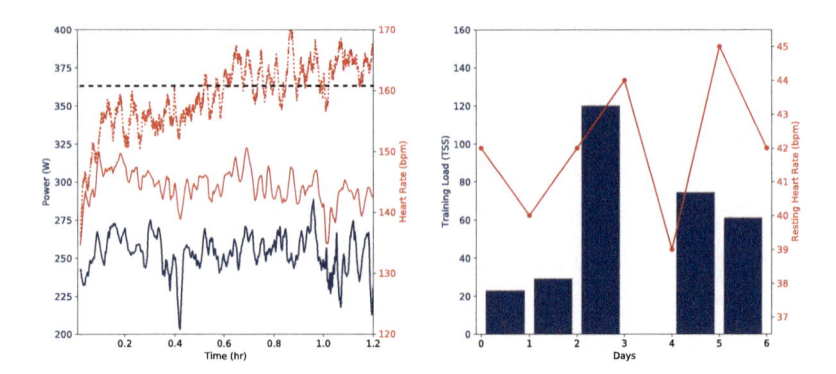

Figure 4.3, left: Same as the right panel of Figure 4.1 but including a hypothetical, critical progression of the heart rate, drawn as a dotted line. The dashed horizontal line illustrates the maximum allowed heart rate in this case. The plot on the right shows an athlete's training load and resting heart rate over the course of a few days.

ceptable one. Let's illustrate this on the same exemplary heat run as before, now using the left panel of Figure 4.3. As already discussed, the measured heart rate (the solid red line) was comparably high in this case. Looking at it more closely, it was elevated from right after the beginning but didn't increase any further. In fact, it even slightly dropped after around one hour despite the essentially unchanged Power level. The fact that it didn't rise any further is a good sign which indicates that the body copes well with the difficult conditions. Though if you observe an ever-increasing heart rate like the hypothetical one drawn with a dotted line in the same graph, you should seriously consider drastically lowering the Power or even canceling the session. What might help in this case is to define a maximum allowed heart rate in advance and take action if this maximum is surpassed. For example, in case the training does not reach beyond the "Tempo" zone 3 (see Section 3.2), your heart rate should usually not surpass ~ 85-87% of your maximum heart rate.

- All forms of stress have an impact on our heart rate, where a higher stress load typically leads to an overall increased heart rate. Forms of stress in this context are manifold, encompassing training, work and personal stress, illness, alcohol consumption, as well as insufficient or bad-quality sleep. All of that affects the body, which is essential to keep in mind for your training schedule. Most training plans are only designed to take into account the training load to achieve a specific goal but, of course, cannot factor in other stress factors. Continuous heart rate monitoring can help you see if you are properly recovering from the various types of stress. A very convenient way to do this is by measuring the resting heart rate (RHR). Most current sports watches with an integrated optical heart-rate sensor automatically calculate the resting heart rate when worn at night, which is what I would recommend doing. Alternatively, with a little more effort, you can manually measure your RHR in the morning right after waking but before getting up. The right panel of Figure 4.3 shows the measured training load as well as the resting heart rate over the course of a few days. Some correlation between the two is visible, especially around the middle of the plot. Here the rest day leads to a very low resting heart rate, thus indicating proper recovery from the day before, which had a higher training load. Through regular RHR monitoring, you should get a good feeling of how your body reacts to different influences. In case you observe an unusual increase, you should try to find out the origin - did you have an intense or long training session? Perhaps a hard day at work? Or are you maybe getting ill? If your RHR is considerably higher than usual, take a critical look at your training schedule and think if it's necessary to revise it. If you have the impression that the rise is not sports-related, taking it a bit easier for a few days is maybe already enough. However, if you can exclude other factors, maybe your overall training load is too high, and you might be at the edge of overtraining. In that case, you should be extremely careful, make sure that you get enough rest, and maybe adapt the plan correspondingly. We will take a closer look at short- and long-term monitoring of training loads in the next section, which helps avoid such situations.

- If you have the impression that your heart rate at a given Power output is consistently lower than it used to be, it could mean that your training has paid off and your state of performance improved. To find out if this is true, just perform an FTP test. The same would be the way to go in the unpleasant situation that your measured heart rate is higher than before at the same Power. Nevertheless, there is no need to be alarmed if this is the case for just a single workout, as we have seen there are many factors that influence the heart rate.

Keeping all this in mind, we will now discuss how to best use the data provided by a running Power meter for training monitoring.

4.2 USING POWER METRICS FOR TRAINING

As you probably have guessed already, making the best out of Power as a training metric means more than merely checking a number on your watch display from time to time. However, there is no need to get nervous; you don't have to be a professional data scientist to train with Power data. This section addresses the utilization of Power and derived quantities at different stages, from direct workout preparation to short- and long-term analysis.

Before a Workout

Let's assume you have a particular workout on your plan. If your Power meter and watch combination allows creating structured, Power-based workouts and uploading them to the watch, then this is undoubtedly the best solution. In case that's not possible, you can still follow structured workouts with just a little more preparation. For one that is easy to remember, you can try to follow it from memory. In case of a more complicated one, an easy workaround should be possible in most cases: If your watch supports structured workouts in general but not yet for Power, there is typically the possibility to add notes to individual workout segments. So defining a workout and just setting the wattage targets as notes should do the trick in this case. As the primary data screen that also works for workouts from memory, I'd generally recommend four fields: Distance, timer, heart rate (either in bpm, percent with respect to the maximum, or zone), and Power - but that's, of course, just personal preference.

Every Power calculation strongly depends on the weight, referring to both the body weight as well as any potential additional load, such as, e.g., the one of a backpack. Make sure that both are adequately set before starting the run. In case your Power meter doesn't allow setting a backpack weight, you might want to consider adjusting your set bodyweight correspondingly.

Several running Power meters offer the possibility to specify the time window over which the calculated values are averaged. The different phases of the running movement actually imply a highly variable Power output. Therefore, the displayed value always has to correspond to the average of at least one running cycle, for example, from one landing with a given foot to the next landing of the same foot. Even if your Power meter (and watch) were capable of measuring and updating the value in real time within a cycle, you wouldn't be able to profit much from it as it'd be constantly fluctuating. Now depending on the type of Power meter, terrain, and workout type, it might be reasonable to set the averaging time higher than the available minimum (which is typically between one and three seconds). As discussed, especially watch-based Power meters are susceptible to time lags of a few seconds because of, e.g., readout of GPS data. However, even acceleration-sensor meters come with an integrated barometric altimeter with a similar reaction time. In the case of a flat course and short-duration intervals, the averaging time is best set close to the minimum, where I'd recommend a value between three and ten seconds. For a workout with less frequent changes or on trails, I generally recommend longer averaging times of 30 - 60 seconds, not least to avoid being unnecessarily distracted by the Power display on the watch, which tends to happen more easily when only the instant value is displayed. Once you've gotten used to your Power meter, you'll likely become better at guessing your Power output without looking at the display and just do so from time to time to calibrate your estimate. Another feature that is offered by some solutions and which helps in this regard is the possibility to update the shown value only every few seconds. In addition to saving watch battery, this helps in conditioning yourself to not look at the display too often, which is also good because it avoids unnecessarily dangerous situations on trails.

In case you want to carry out the planned workout on trails or in the mountains (or both), you should think beforehand if it is feasible to run the selected route at the intended Power levels. This refers to downhill and technical sections where trying to reach or stay at a certain Power level can be dangerous. If you really want to carry out a specific workout but are unsure if it is feasible on the intended course, it might be a good idea to rethink the route choice.

During the Workout

Assuming you followed all the outlined preparation steps, you are set for the training and should be able to carry it out without too much additional effort. From time to time and when safely possible, check the data screen of your watch and compare the Power value to the respective goal. Although you should try to reach and hold the target value, variations or discrepancies of a few percent are expected because of uncertainties and thus unproblematic. So the general goal is to follow the prescribed Power values of the workout, but only to the extent that it is compatible with the terrain and your capabilities. Always remember that not being able to train because of an injury is definitely much more inefficient than running a section of a single run at a lower intensity than planned!

As already discussed, monitoring the heart rate during a run provides additional helpful information, allowing you to take action if you don't yet realize or admit that a particular effort might be too much on a given day, be it because of weather conditions or your own form.

Analysis

Up to now, we have only looked at how a Power meter can be used for an individual workout. However, efficient training means planning and putting every session into a bigger picture, taking into account both the short- and long-term response of an athlete's body. The Power-based training metrics introduced earlier are very well suited for that purpose. Regarding the corresponding analysis, some training platforms have it included as part of their membership, but usually not for free. So in case you are happy with, e.g., the standard workout analysis that comes with the app of your sports watch and don't want to spend ~ 10-15$ per month for an additional membership, you might be glad to hear that there is a free alternative. All you need for an elementary but efficient analysis is basic spreadsheet knowledge and the motivation to enter the relevant information into a table after each workout. Then again, several reasons also speak in favor of such a paid subscription, such as convenience, more in-depth analysis, and the advantage of having everything at the same place. Just be aware that the proper usage of Power data doesn't automatically imply that you have to pay something, especially since the fundamental part of the analysis consists of rather simple calculations. An example of such a self-implemented analysis is shown in Figure 4.4. Every row corresponds to a specific workout, and different types of sports are included, all of them carried out with a Power meter. Assuming that proper FTP values were set for the running and cycling Power meters, TSS values

DATE	TYPE	DURATION	IF	TIF	TSS	VI	CTL	ATL	ATL/CTL	COMMENTS
8/6	Trail	21.75	0.64	0.98	894.30	1.09	104.55	169.90	1.63	Ultra Race
8/5	Trail	0.55	0.69	0.64	25.90	1.01	86.31	52.86	0.61	
8/3	Cycling	0.52	0.74	0.68	27.90	1.10	89.94	58.37	0.65	
8/1	Hiking	1.2	0.56	0.57	52.00		94.44	85.61	0.91	
7/31	Cycling	2	0.64	0.70						
7/31	Hiking	0.8	0.51	0.49						
7/30	Cycling	2.1	0.63	0.69						
7/29	Cycling	1.65	0.67	0.71						
7/28	Cycling	1.6	0.63	0.67						
7/26	Trail	2.6	0.75	0.86						
7/25	Cycling	1.5	0.64	0.68						
7/24	Flat	1.6	0.85	0.91						
7/22	Trail	2	0.76	0.84						

Figure 4.4: Example of a self-generated analysis spreadsheet. The cutout shown here documents the final preparation for an ultra-trail race. The inlay corresponds to the performance management chart for the given period, i.e., the evolution of ATL and CTL.

were calculated for all activities, allowing it to compare and accumulate the corresponding training loads consistently. If no TSS is available for a workout, there are several ways to estimate a corresponding value. Some training platforms and sports watches use an algorithm that combines the durations spent in different heart-rate zones to a quantity called hrTSS (see, e.g., reference 11). In case you have an hrTSS for an activity without a TSS calculation, you can use it as a replacement. In case you don't but still recorded your heart rate during the training, you can estimate the TSS from the average heart rate HR_{avg} and the workout duration t in units of hours with the following formula:

$$\text{TSS}_{est,HR} = \left(\text{HR}_{avg}/\text{HR}_{thresh}\right)^3 \cdot t \cdot 100 \approx \left(1.13 \cdot \text{HR}_{avg}/\text{HR}_{max}\right)^3 \cdot t \cdot 100,$$

where HR_{thresh} corresponds to your heart rate at threshold pace and HR_{max} to the maximum one. Here are two examples for calculating the estimated TSS:

- The average heart rate during an activity with a duration of 1.5 hours was 140 bpm. In the case of a threshold heart rate of 170 bpm, this yields
$$\text{TSS}_{est} = (140/170)^3 \cdot 1.5 \cdot 100 = 0.82^3 \cdot 1.5 \cdot 100 = 0.56 \cdot 1.5 \cdot 100 = \underline{83.8}$$
- The average heart rate was 70% of the maximum for a workout duration of 3 hours. This gives
$$\text{TSS}_{est} = (1.13 \cdot 0.70)^3 \cdot 3 \cdot 100 = \underline{148.5}$$

For activities with neither Power nor heart-rate data, a rough estimate can still be made using the perceived effort of the activity (reference 12).

This Rating of Perceived Exertion (RPE) is a scale from 1 to 10, where values of 1 are assigned to activities with minimal exertion and 10 to those at maximum effort. The estimated reference TSS is given in Table 4.1. Originally, this reference was supposed to be scaled linearly with the activity duration in hours for the TSS estimation. Here I propose a revised calculation that should lead to more realistic results for longer activities:

$$\text{TSS}_{est,RPE} = \text{TSS}_{ref} \cdot t^{3/4}$$

Let's again illustrate this on two examples:

- A three-hour race at maximum effort would likely be rated with an RPE of 9 or 10. If it is 10, then we get
$$\text{TSS}_{est,RPE} = 100 \cdot 3^{3/4} = 100 \cdot 2.28 = \underline{228}.$$

RPE	1	2	3	4	5	6	7	8	9	10
TSS$_{ref}$	10	20	30	50	60	80	85	90	95	100

Table 4.1: Estimated reference TSS, depending on the Rating of Perceived Exertion. Inspired from the table within reference 12 but adapted for the modified calculation introduced in the text.

- For a 90-minute training run with RPE $= 4$, the estimated TSS is $TSS_{est,RPE} = 50 \cdot 1.5^{3/4} = 50 \cdot 1.36 = \underline{67.8}$.

Given that the RPE is an entirely subjective measure, results vary strongly from athlete to athlete and also depend on the form of the day. For a combined training analysis together with "real" (Power-calculated) TSS values, I'd thus recommend only using the RPE-estimated TSS when unavoidable, i.e., when no heart-rate data is available.

For activities where an estimated TSS is used (regardless if it is hrTSS, $TSS_{est,HR}$, or $TSS_{est,RPE}$), a corresponding estimated intensity factor can be calculated via

$$IF_{est} = \sqrt{\frac{TSS}{100 \cdot t}},$$

where t again denotes the duration in hours. For our last TSS estimation example ($TSS_{est,RPE} = 67.8$ and 90 minutes duration), this gives

$$IF_{est} = \sqrt{67.8/(100 \cdot 1.5)} = \sqrt{0.45} = \underline{0.67}.$$

Coming back to the workout analysis, the key values to be entered in the table (see Figure 4.4) are the type of sport, the activity duration, TSS and IF (measured or estimated), and (optionally and if available) the VI. The software can automatically calculate the TIF from the IF and the duration. The same applies to two TSS-derived quantities, the acute and the chronic training load (ATL and CTL, see reference 13). Both are defined as the average TSS load per day over a preceding period, which is one week for the ATL and six weeks for the CTL. The idea behind these two quantities is to monitor both the short- and longer-term strain, which is very helpful for evaluating if the amount of training load is appropriate at a given stage of the training. The pure CTL (six weeks averaging) quantifies how much training stress an athlete is currently accustomed to. In relation to it, the ATL (one week averaging) tells if the short-term load corresponds to a relaxed, regular, or an intense training phase. Continuously evaluating these two variables allows setting training stimuli, avoiding overtraining, and recovering just the right amount to reach peak form on race day. Probably the best presentation of the evolution of CTL and ATL is via a chart where both are plotted as a function of time (see inlay of Figure 4.4).

This is often called the Performance Management Chart (PMC), but to avoid you having to remember more acronyms than necessary, we'll keep referring to it as the ATL-CTL chart (or similar). The same applies to a quantity that is often plotted together in this chart, the so-called Training Stress Balance (TSB). It simply corresponds to the difference between CTL and ATL. By definition, positive values correspond to more relaxed and negative ones to more intense training phases, and 0 to a balance between the short- and mid-term training load. It is certainly good to keep an eye on the difference between CTL and ATL for properly directing the training, which is especially helpful to avoid overtraining. Many references go a step further and even provide recommended values of the CTL-ATL difference for the tapering phase right before a race to achieve maximum performance. Be careful as these numbers are typically not designed for ultra-endurance athletes. CTL and ATL values can reach 100 or more when preparing for an ultra run because of the high training volume (see also Figure 4.4), which is generally more than when preparing for a shorter race. If you'd lower the ATL only by a fixed value that has not been adjusted to the high CTL, you're risking carrying residual fatigue into the race. For that reason, I'd recommend looking less at the absolute difference of CTL and ATL and more at the ratio of ATL/CTL. The table in Figure 4.4 contains the ATL/CTL ratio values as a separate column, where values above 1.00 correspond to more intense training phases and vice versa. Of course, the CTL-ATL difference can also be added, but for many athletes it might also be sufficient to just read the rough number directly from the chart.

5 - RACE PREPARATION

I still vividly remember the beginning of my first ultra trail race. It started with a flat segment, first running through a village near the Austrian-German border and then entering a forest at the bottom of a mountain. This is where the first ascent of that course began. Almost everybody knew that it would take a while and thus tried to settle into it and find a good rhythm. That's when I noticed a runner standing at the side, being completely exhausted, bent over the poles, and panting for breath. The scene appeared as if it happened near the end or after the finish line - But it did after barely 10% of the total race, referring to both distance and altitude gain. Surely there might be other explanations for this individual situation than catastrophic over-pacing. Still, it's just the most extreme example of what I've observed many times, equally on others and myself: Many (if not even most) runners don't know how to pace during a race. In most cases, this leads to starting too fast, followed by unnecessarily quick and strong exhaustion. For road races without significant inclines, this can be prevented by sticking to a previously defined, realistic target pace. However, this approach is not feasible for trail races due to obvious reasons. Heart-rate-based pacing improves the situation, but apart from the already mentioned caveats, one additional important factor affects many runners during a race, especially at the beginning: Excitement. Having prepared for that moment for several months or even years and finally standing at the starting line while anticipating what might come releases adrenaline. While this process has many benefits, one of the side effects of adrenaline is an increased heart rate. Knowing about this only partly helps because it can easily happen that an elevated heart rate (with respect to the goal) is falsely blamed entirely on excitement. Perhaps you have already experienced this yourself: You are at the starting line together with your competitors, waiting for the race to begin. The organizers are playing a rock classic at full volume to heat up the crowd. While preparing your watch for recording, you realize that your heart rate is much higher than before all your training runs. It's only reasonable to think you cannot rely on it and instead use something else to base your pacing on. The natural choice for this alternative is your perception, and this is where you walk into the trap: Because of all the excitement, you'll likely feel great at the beginning of the race, running faster than you planned and seemingly without effort. The problem is that you are being tricked by yourself, and while everything seems to go easy at this stage, be assured that you'll have to pay double the prize for exaggerating later on. If only there were a better way to control your pace! There is, and as you have likely already guessed by now, it is Power. By not only training but also racing with a running Power meter, you can monitor your exerted effort objectively right from the beginning, being able to control yourself when you can't rely on internal values like heart rate or feeling. However, a Power meter itself is useless if you don't have a pacing/

Power strategy, which can make the difference between a successful finish and a dissatisfying DNF. The question that comes naturally is:

What Power level is feasible for the race I want to run?

The (admittedly ambitious) objective of this chapter is to describe a universal, Power-based approach that allows you to not only properly prepare for a specific race but also develop a custom strategy to run it at your maximum potential. In case you've signed up for a long and technical trail race with many ascents and descents, you're probably skeptical that it's even possible to write down a generic procedure that describes at how much Power you should run it. Let me try to convince you of the opposite: While there are naturally some details to consider, the key aspects of the concept are not really complicated. We will go through everything step by step and summarize it at the end.

5.1 SETTING THE GOAL

Before thinking about the actual preparation and the development of the racing strategy, you first need to find the answer to the following fundamental question:

What finishing time is realistic?

It is effectively the starting point for every dedicated preparation, laying the foundation for everything which comes afterwards. The duration of an activity is the main characteristic that determines which maximum effort an athlete can perform. While this sounds plausible and natural, it is still worth thinking about it a little. Most races are designed to finish a specific route or distance as quickly as possible, and we are thus used to compare runners by how fast they can finish it. While there is nothing to complain about here, this approach of comparing performances artificially enhances the apparent discrepancy between athletes of different levels. Let's illustrate this on a marathon runner with a finishing time of 4 hours. When asked to compare this result to the one of a world-class marathon runner who only needs around 2 hours to complete that distance, many people would likely answer that the elite athlete runs twice as fast as the amateur. It's a very simple calculation, so it has to be correct, right? Well, yes and no. It is indeed true that the average speed of the world-class runner is twice as high during the race, but that still does not mean that he generally runs twice as fast as the amateur. Despite the same route, distance, and other conditions, the two athletes effectively run two completely different races. The elite runner knows very well how fast it is possible to finish and can therefore perform at a much higher intensity. A more even comparison between the two would be to check their covered distance in a race with a fixed duration. In the case of two hours, basically nothing changes for the elite runner, whereas the amateur could run this race at a higher speed. Conversely, for a fixed duration of four hours, nothing changes for the amateur, but the high-performance athlete has to adapt to a duration that is twice as long as what he is used to. There is likely not a single world-class marathon runner who is used to such race durations, so even such a highly trained individual would have to adapt the training accordingly beforehand for best results. The bottom line is: When it comes to preparing for a race, try to avoid thinking of it in terms of distance or altitude gain, but rather focus your training and race strategy on the expected duration.

A good time to deal with the question of the expected duration is around two to three months before the competition takes place. The remaining time frame allows for good race-specific preparation, assuming that you have been training appropriately beforehand. Earlier in the season, you can focus on improving your speed basis as well as specifics such as technical sections, downhill running, etc. At that stage, you can surely already try to estimate how fast you might be able to finish. However, I'd highly recommend carrying out the final assessment not too early as your capabilities still evolve over a longer period of time.

What's tacitly assumed throughout this section is that the race you've signed up for is feasible for you. This not only encompasses that you feel physically capable of running the given course, including its potential technical challenges, but also that you've given your body enough time to adapt to the corresponding terrain and especially to running longer distances. The human body is relatively quick in building up muscles, and also the cardiovascular system re-

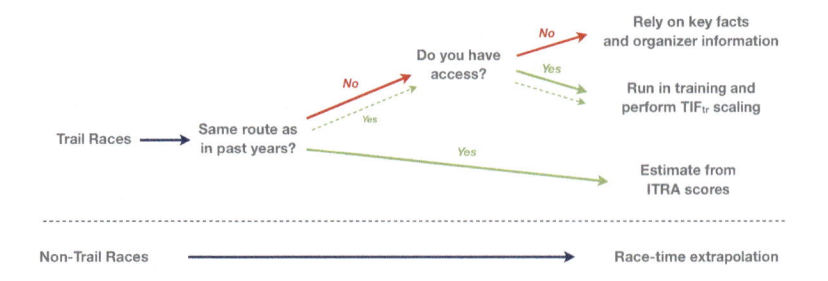

Figure 5.1: Sketch of different approaches to estimate a realistic finishing time for races that are run for the first time as explained in the text.

acts quite well to training stimuli. The fact that these adaptation processes are fast is dangerous for running newcomers. Often they increase intensity and volume too quickly, which is problematic because tendons and ligaments adjust much more slowly, typically on timescales of months up to years. I would therefore recommend not increasing the maximum race distance by more than a factor of two each year. For example, if you're used to half-marathon races and want to go for longer distances, it's better to first prepare for a marathon the following year and leave the ultra distances to the subsequent years.

Now back to the key question of estimating a realistic finishing time. The most straightforward situation would be a race which you've already finished and want to run again. Considering how well you raced that day and how your general form has developed since then, you likely already have a good feeling about what you can achieve next time. As for courses where you can't bring in past racing experience, several cases are to be discussed, for which an overview is given in Figure 5.1.

Let's first talk about trail races. The pitfall when trying to estimate how long it takes to finish an unknown trail-running race is that often one just looks at the elementary key facts: distance and altitude gain/loss. However, it is usually more complicated than this. Amount and difficulty of technical sections, steepness of ascents and descents, altitude, and weather conditions all affect the overall running speed. Even when you are fully aware of that, it can still easily happen that you are misestimating their importance, and often this will be an underestimation. It is therefore essential to include as much additional information as possible. Sometimes the organizer not only provides cutoff times but also estimated race times for runners with different levels to help with the self-assessment. If nothing better is available, these can be used as a compromise. The possibilities for better estimating the duration firstly depend on if the route is the same as in previous race editions and secondly if you have access to it and can thus run it as part of your training. In case the answer to both is no, you don't have much choice but to work out an estimate based on what was already mentioned before (distance, altitude profile, and organizer information). However, when you have the possibility to run the route as part of your training, you benefit from it in several ways. In addition to a better race-time estimation, getting to know the different sections directly brings a mental advantage for the race since you know what awaits you. So how is it now possible to calculate a realistic race duration from these training run(s)? In Section 3.3, the TIF was introduced as a quantity that characterizes the intensity of a workout relative to the possible maximum for the given duration. Since the target intensity for a race is precisely this achievable maximum, the TIF is thus ideally suited to assess how long it takes to finish a competition when having trained on it beforehand. If the route is short enough such that you don't have to split it up and complete it in one training, the estimated race duration can be calculated via:

$$t_{est,race} = t_{tr} \cdot TIF_{tr},$$

where t_{tr} corresponds to the time it took to finish the route in the training and TIF_{tr} to the time-corrected intensity factor of this run. As an example, let's assume that the test run lasted four hours and was carried out with IF = 0.70. With $IF_{max}(4\,h) = 0.83$ (see Figure 3.3), the corresponding time-corrected intensity factor is $TIF_{tr} = 0.70/0.83 = 0.84$. This means that this training run was performed at roughly 84% of the maximum achievable intensity for this duration, whereas the race would be carried out with TIF = 1.00. According to the formula above, we then get $t_{est,race} = 4\,h \cdot 0.84 = 3.36\,h \approx 3\,h\,22\,min$. It has to be noted that this is just meant to provide an estimate and is thus not exact for several reasons. First of all, we have already seen that while a higher Power output leads to a faster running speed, the correlation is not entirely linear. In other words, increasing the Power by, e.g., 10% does not exactly lead to a 10% faster speed, although the scaling is still not too inaccurate. Secondly, here we simply scaled the time of the training run with a TIF that has also been calculated using the duration of the same run (4 h in our case), although IF_{max} is actually higher for the race because of the shorter duration (approximately 3 h 22 min). Luckily both effects work against each other and should thus cancel out to a certain degree. A more important factor that influences the final race result is your overall form. Both the training that comes after the assessment as well as your daily form on race day finally determine what is possible, which can lead to either a slower or a faster result. Keeping these caveats in mind, the calculation can be extended to longer routes which are split up into several training runs. Since these different splits are generally not run at the same intensity, it is first necessary to calculate an average IF as well as the total duration of all runs:

$$IF_{avg} = \frac{IF_1 \cdot t_1 + IF_2 \cdot t_2 + \ldots}{t_1 + t_2 + \ldots}, \quad t_{tot} = t_1 + t_2 + \ldots,$$

where each index stands for one split. The total duration is then used to look up $IF_{max}(t_{tot})$, which in turn allows calculating $TIF_{tr} = IF_{avg}/IF_{max}(t_{tot})$. Similarly to above, the estimated race time is then

$$t_{est,race} = t_{tot} \cdot TIF_{tr}.$$

Let's again illustrate the calculation with an example where the route was split into three runs with the following durations and intensities:

- $t_1 = 1.5\,\text{h}$, $\text{IF}_1 = 0.85$
- $t_2 = 2.5\,\text{h}$, $\text{IF}_2 = 0.77$
- $t_3 = 2\,\text{h}$, $\text{IF}_3 = 0.80$

This yields $t_{tot} = 6\,\text{h}$ and

$$\text{IF}_{avg} = \frac{0.85 \cdot 1.5\,\text{h} + 0.77 \cdot 2.5\,\text{h} + 0.80 \cdot 2\,\text{h}}{6\,\text{h}} = 0.80.$$

According to the IF_{max} calculation and Figure 3.3, $\text{IF}_{max}(6\,\text{h}) = 0.78$, and therefore $\text{TIF}_{tr} = 0.80/0.78 \approx 1.03$. Time-corrected intensity factors are usually not higher than 1.00, however in this case the value is still correct because it was calculated by combining several shorter runs. The estimated race duration is $t_{est,race} = 6\,\text{h} \cdot 1.03 \approx 6\,\text{h}\,10\,\text{min}$ and therefore even slightly longer than the sum of the duration of the training runs because of their comparably high intensity.

If the route of this trail race is unchanged with respect to the previous years and assuming that you have already participated in other trail races, there is another, quite elegant way of estimating a realistic race duration. The International Trail Running Association (ITRA, webpage itra.run) hosts a database with the ambition to collect and compare the race results of as many trail runners as possible. The collected results are automatically analyzed with an algorithm that considers the route characteristics and assigns a performance index, the so-called ITRA score. Values of this score range from 0 to 1000, where a higher number denotes a better result. The different recent scores of a runner are averaged according to a specific weighting system, providing one overall runner performance index, which is also a value with the same rating between 0 and 1000. Looking up the performance index of any runner that is cataloged by the ITRA is free, whereas the detailed breakdown that also includes the individual race scores is only available for ITRA members. Given the sophistication of the ITRA score calculation, an athlete's ITRA performance index is a very helpful tool to compare different runners and can thus also be used for estimating the time it might take you to finish a particular race. This can be done as follows: First, look up yourself on the webpage and check your performance index. If no value is displayed, it is likely that your races could not be appropriately categorized or that no ITRA score calculation was possible. In this case, you can still try to check the performance indices of friends and roughly estimate your own index from these. The next step is to look for past results of the race you want to run, which are in many cases linked on the event's webpage. Then it is rather straightforward: Just search for the ITRA performance indices of a few runners that have already finished this race. The correlation of their indices with their finishing times combined with your own performance index should give you a good feeling of what is possible. This approach works best for races with many finishers because then individual fluctuations can be better averaged out. Furthermore, if you are confident that your performance index has improved compared to the races it has been evaluated from, it is justified to be a bit more optimistic.

The last case to be discussed refers to non-trail races. The absence of technical sections and the generally lower amount of altitude change for this race type allow estimating finishing times by extrapolating results from other (mostly shorter) distances, henceforth called reference distance. Such a reference distance d_{ref} can, for example, be a half or a full marathon. Together with the corresponding duration t_{ref}, the estimated time t for the distance d can be calculated as follows:

$$t = t_{\text{ref}} \cdot \left(\frac{d}{d_{\text{ref}}}\right)^{1.20}.$$

This function is directly derived from a simplified version of the running-Power calculation described in chapter 2 and the $IF_{\max}$ calculation from Section 3.3 (I'll spare you the mathematical details). It has to be noted that this general functional relation has already been empirically obtained by Peter Riegel (reference 14) by comparing world records set at different distances. The only but important difference with respect to the above formula is that he obtained an exponent of 1.06 instead of 1.20 above. The used value determines the assumed level of fatigue. For trained athletes, Riegel's value is generally valid for durations up to around three to four hours. In contrast, for longer durations (so generally to most readers of this book), I'd recommend using the formula as it is given above. The main reasons for

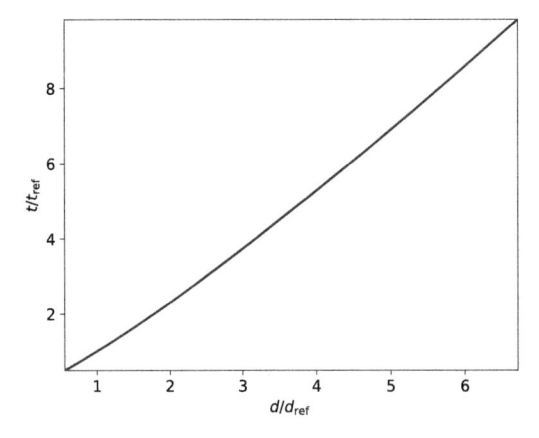

d/d_{ref}	t/t_{ref}
50 / 42.2	1.23
2	2.30
100 / 42.2	2.82
161 / 42.2	4.99
200 / 42.2	6.47

Figure 5.2: Race-time scaling for flat, non-trail races as a function of the distance ratio. The graph on the left shows the continuous function over a wider range, whereas specific scaling values are shown on the table on the right side.

the quicker exhaustion towards longer durations are the change of the primary energy supply source from carbohydrates to fat as well as a gradual decline of the running form.

The obtained functional relation is plotted and evaluated for a few common examples in Figure 5.2. For four out of five examples, the reference distance is $d_{ref} = 42.2$, the length of a marathon in units of km. This table might thus come in handy for marathon runners aiming for common ultra distances, such as 50 km, 100 km, 100 miles (roughly 161 km), or even 200 km. Let's illustrate the usage of this relation on a runner with a marathon time of $t_{ref} = 3\,\text{h}$ who wants to run a race with $d = 100\,\text{km}$. The scaling factor is, in this case, $t/t_{\text{ref}} = 2.82$, and the estimated feasible duration is thus $t = 2.82 \cdot 3\,\text{h} = 8.46\,\text{h} \approx 8\,\text{h}\,30\,\text{min}$. It is important to mention that, like for all other approaches outlined in this section, finishing a race at the estimated time still requires dedicated preparation. Extrapolating a marathon result to 100 km not only involves an uncertainty but also requires a different training approach, as will be discussed later.

Now assuming that you have estimated a realistic finishing time for your race using at least one of the methods described above, you are ready for the next step: Calculating the target Power. As already discussed in Section 3.3 and again before introducing the TIF_{tr}-based time estimate, the duration of an activity determines what maximum intensity factor IF_{max} is reachable. While the actual IF is and should be below this achievable maximum during training, the goal for a race is to actually reach it. Together with the FTP, the expected duration thus allows calculating the goal for the normalized Power. As for race durations up to around three to four hours, it is given via

$$\text{NP}_{\text{race,shorter}} = \text{FTP} \cdot \text{IF}_{\text{max}}(t) = \text{FTP} \cdot t^{-0.0566}.$$

The applied exponent was obtained by using the above-mentioned, empirically obtained exponent from Peter Riegel's time-distance scaling and reverting it to Power. In case of longer durations, I'd recommend using

$$\text{NP}_{\text{race,longer}} = \text{FTP} \cdot \text{IF}_{\text{max}}(t) = \text{FTP} \cdot t^{-0.1383}\text{ instead.}$$

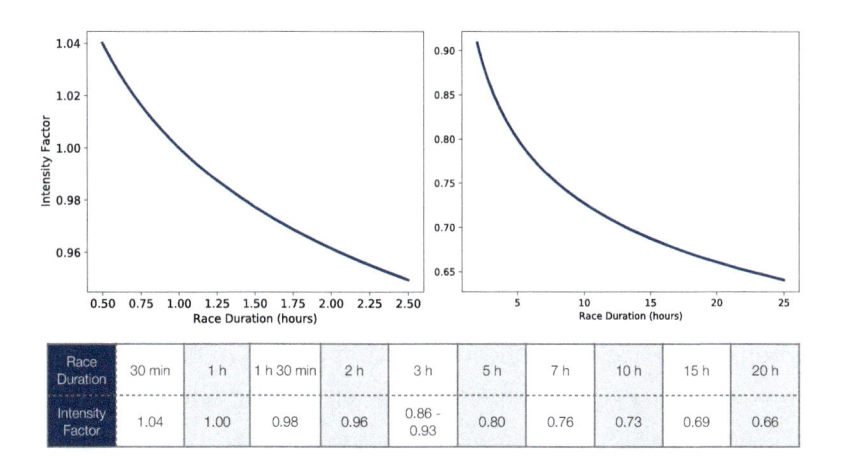

Race Duration	30 min	1 h	1 h 30 min	2 h	3 h	5 h	7 h	10 h	15 h	20 h
Intensity Factor	1.04	1.00	0.98	0.96	0.86 - 0.93	0.80	0.76	0.73	0.69	0.66

Figure 5.3: Goal Intensity Factor as a function of the expected race duration for shorter (upper left) and longer (upper right) races. The table gives values for specific discrete race durations.

The target for the IF is given in Figure 5.3 for race durations up to 25 hours, effectively complementing Figure 3.3 to longer durations. Knowing in advance what IF_{max} or respectively NP_{race} to aim for implies a considerable advantage both for the preparation as well as the race itself. It greatly helps to plan the race-specific training and allows developing a race strategy that maximizes the athlete's potential - more about that in the coming sections.

Seeing how the IF_{max} calculation is displayed up to race durations of 25 hours, you are perhaps skeptical about the general validity of the presented approach. Many ultra runners have the habit of always setting their training focus on long runs with low intensity and simultaneously avoiding shorter workouts at or even above FTP level. To those, the concept of calculating the Power for an ultra race based on the maximum possible effort for only one hour probably does not appear reasonable. If you belong to this runner type, you are probably hard to convince of the following: To become a faster ultra runner does *not* mean that you should only train long distances and always run at low or moderate intensity. There is a solid correlation between short-, medium-, and long-distance performances, leaving out very short efforts below one minute. Let's say we observe two ultra runners who completed the same non-trail 100 k race, one with a time of 7 h 30 min and the other one in 9 h, where we are assuming that both paced their race reasonably. If both athletes would, after an appropriate recovery time, compete together at a 5 k race, the chances of the 9-h runner to beat the other one even at this completely different distance are still rather low. This correlation between reachable speeds/Power for endurance activities is not a coincidence. In simplified terms, the maximum Power you can achieve over a certain duration is determined by two factors: Your general Power level, which is characterized by the FTP, and the level of fatigue. It is therefore generally advisable to implement training phases with shorter runs of medium and high intensity, such as a half-marathon training plan, to boost the FTP and thus your general Power level. If you do so, you are, in fact, in good company. World-class ultra runners like Kilian Jornet or Jim Walmsley incorporate interval sessions and threshold runs in their training, knowing of their value for their general speed. Dedicated training phases with a focus on shorter durations usually fit well into the off-season, although it makes sense to integrate corresponding workouts (e.g., fartleks) also into training plans for longer distances. Apart from these short workouts, the focus on higher training volume at a lower intensity of such a plan ensures that the athlete is trained to endure the expected duration at optimum performance, minimizing the level of unnecessary fatigue. This final adaptation corresponds to the race-specific preparation, which typically starts around three months before the race.

Although the presented functional relation for IF_{max} can naturally slightly deviate from runner to runner, it should still correspond to a reliable guideline. Most importantly, I'd highly recommend never to start mistrusting this relation at the beginning of a race and then fall into the previously described "feel-good" trap. The chances of regretting this later on are very high. However, there is one exception where the t-IF_{max} relation cannot be applied in a straightforward manner anymore. In the case of races that are split into several stages, sleep additionally complicates the situation. Because of this intermediate recovery, a hypothetical IF_{max} value that is calculated from the total expected race duration would be too pessimistic. Then again, the different stages can also not be treated fully independently. Though the first stage can generally be run at IF_{max}, this is undoubtedly not ideal either because it would lead to excessive exhaustion, which is hard to recover from on short timescales. Therefore, the optimum lies somewhere in between, but it is hard to give a general prescription for properly scaling the target intensity in this case. Relevant factors are the average stage duration, the recovery time between them, and the overall number of stages. Furthermore, the general ability to recover also plays a role. For an actual stage race that lasts between a few days and a week and with individual durations of up to several hours, it is possible to base the IF_{max} calculation on the expected daily duration and scale the value(s) down by a given percentage, where a value of around 5% should work well in many cases. As an example, if you expect a typical stage duration of 5 hours, the modified target IF would lie at 0.76 instead of the nominal 0.80. However, this approach is not viable for extreme ultra races that are not split into several parts and which are too long to be finished without sleep, say with a duration of 30 hours or longer. Here the recovery time is usually minimized to optimize the running time. For this race type, the target intensity should rather be oriented on the rough total duration and then be slightly scaled up. Then again, a too specific target intensity is probably overstated in this case anyway; the greatest use of it is perhaps that it can serve as a guideline at the beginning of the race to settle into a good rhythm.

5.2 PREPARING

Although it may not seem like it, the efforts to estimate the expected race duration and calculate the corresponding target IF in the previous section are not only relevant for the race itself but also determine the preparation beforehand. This race-specific training should ideally start around 12 weeks before the event, although it can also be reduced to 8 weeks with a proper focus and good training foundation. Going for a shorter phase makes sense when, for example, you have several races on your calendar. We are going to discuss both scenarios. Especially if your main race is a challenging, long ultra race, you should make sure that you are entering the specific preparatory phase already with a good foundation and such that your body is used to a higher chronic training load. This is naturally even more important if you choose a shorter dedicated preparation (8 weeks in our case), but it should be obvious that ultra running is nothing that should be started from scratch with only a few months of lead time.

Essentially, race-specific training means preparing the athlete to run for a particular duration at a given intensity. This duration is the estimated time it takes to finish the race, and the intensity is the corresponding IF_{max}. Now one might say "alright fair enough, so I'll just run the expected duration at target intensity from time to time and am perfectly prepared, right?". As you probably expect, the answer is a clear no. This approach would mean that the training would entirely consist of simulated races. Aside from not being realizable for longer races or even generally because of the lack of adrenaline, it is simply not efficient because of the unnecessarily long recovery. Instead, a dedicated preparation revolves around a Power that corresponds to $IF_{max} \cdot FTP$, at the same time prepares the athlete for the race duration, and ensures to do both without exaggerating. Generally speaking, training means setting a stimulus with the intention to throw the body out of balance in a controlled manner and thus trigger adaptation processes of the organism. The goal of a training plan is then to find the appropriate combination and amount of workouts to optimize these adaptation processes while giving the body enough time to recover and improve. You probably already suspect that finding the perfect balance to maximize a runner's potential is a complex problem. A proper custom-tailored training plan needs to take into account the specifics of a runner, and a generic prescription like the one that is going to follow can, therefore, not replace a personal trainer. Having said that, there is still a lot you can achieve by training yourself. Either way, maybe the most important advice is to not blindly follow a plan but always listen to your body. Overambition can be dangerous, and repetitively ignoring relevant signs bears the danger of overtraining or other injuries. Acting accordingly by lowering the training volume or intensity as well as alternate forms of training should help overcome such a difficult phase. A helpful way of checking your body's response to training and other stress is monitoring the resting heart rate, as was already discussed in more detail in Section 4.1.

As already said, the target Power during the race plays an important role also for the preparation. For medium and longer races, it comprises the central part of the specific training phase, whereas the contribution is lower for shorter ones with a correspondingly higher IF_{max}. Spending a large amount of the training time in this zone is naturally effective as it ensures that the body gets used to it. Although the concept may sound obvious, it is still worth keeping in mind. For example, let's take the preparation for an ultra run with an expected duration of 7 hours, corresponding to an IF_{max} of 0.76 (see Figure 5.3). An important part of the preparation of such a race are long runs with a duration of 3 hours and more. Many runners would likely run these at a certain "standard" long-run intensity, which is (and should) for most correspond to a Power lower than 76% of the FTP. Forcing the Power up to 76% FTP for the entire run might, in this case, already cause an unnecessary high training load. In that situation, a good solution for many is a variable long run (see the workout "Long Run with Variation" in Section 6.1), where the Power is varied between the race target Power and a more relaxed one from time to time. Such a workout sets a very productive, race-specific training stimulus and should avoid excessive exhaustion if adequately scheduled and carried out. Although the general focus during these last weeks before the event lies on the target Power, it is essential to include different types of workouts that target various Power zones. Runners of shorter races profit from long runs at lower Power in terms of basic endurance, whereas runs at higher intensity prevent extensive monotony for ultra runners.

In case the upcoming event is a trail or a mountain race, the time ahead of it should not only be used to build up the necessary endurance but also to specifically train for what awaits you. Depending on the race, this can cover many aspects. Maybe most important are ascents and descents. Uphill and downhill running stresses muscles differently than flat terrain, which needs to be specifically trained, ideally starting already before the race-specific preparation. If possible, the overall proportion of ascents and descents with respect to the distance in training should be at a similar level as for the race. In addition to that, the total amount of altitude gain in the peak training week should be at least as high as the one that will be accomplished during the race (reference 15). In the event that you do not have the luxury of living in the mountains, there are several ways to minimize the resulting disadvantage. One possibility for mimicking uphill running is to run on a treadmill that is set to a particular incline. Another one is to transfer some workouts onto the bicycle. Cycling is, in fact, very similar to uphill running and hiking in terms of muscular activity, which makes it an excellent alternative sport, especially for trail and mountain runners. Particularly worth emphasizing in this regard are indoor trainers with the capability to measure the Power output and dynamically adjust the resistance to enforce a prescribed Power, called smart trainers. Investing the money and space (if available) in such a setup can greatly pay off, especially in the winter season or in case of certain injuries which prevent running but still admit to cycle. The integrated Power measurement allows combining training load etc. consistently to the running workouts, naturally on condition that the respective FTP is set correctly. In addition to that, structured exercises improve the training quality and ensure an appropriate intensity level. Apart from training for uphill and downhill sections, other factors to consider including in the specific preparation are for example:

- Technical sections - Trail runs require modifying the running style and dedicated training, which should ideally be part of the general training routine. This triggers physical adaptation processes of muscles, tendons, and ligaments and also trains the needed coordination. Despite all these advantages, it might be worth considering to avoid overly technical or risky parts in the final two to three weeks before the race to minimize the risk of an acute injury.

- Nutrition - This is an important topic, especially for ultra runners. For shorter and medium-distance races, no or only slight fueling with carbohydrates such as in the form of gels should be sufficient. For longer races, the composition of the food intake should generally include more and more solid food with other energy sources, such as proteins and fat. Especially the longer training runs are well suited to test what works best for you and, in turn, to find out what might cause problems.

- **Running with a backpack** - The equipment for most trail races, as required by the organizer, makes carrying a running backpack indispensable for medium and longer distances. Getting used to this additional weight should be trained beforehand. Using a backpack for the long runs is an excellent way to do so as it not only prepares your upper body for it but also ensures that you get used to accessing different items, ideally even without stopping. Just keep in mind to enter the additional weight in your Power meter settings. A further key aspect whose importance goes far beyond backpack running is complementary strength training, which is, for example, nicely discussed in the books by Paul Hobrough (references 16 and 17).

- **Running with a headlamp** - Obviously, this only becomes relevant for races that take place at least partly at night. Especially on the trails but even on technically unchallenging terrain, running with a headlamp is something that is definitely worth getting used to beforehand.

- **Flat running** - Many trail runners dislike road running and therefore run on trails and in the mountains as much as possible. However, even those who only sign up for technical trail races can still benefit from conducting part of their training on the road. While having to continuously adapt the running style on uneven terrain usually has to be considered an advantage of trail running, the monotony of road running allows to develop and maintain an efficient running form. Additionally, holding and adapting a prescribed Power level is generally easier on the road.

- **Mental training** - Last but not least, psychological preparation is crucial, especially for ultra runners. The immense physical effort also challenges our brain, making us think about stopping when it feels particularly hard. A proper pacing strategy as described in this chapter can help minimize such lows, but still, be prepared that essentially every ultra race brings its ups and downs. There are several ways of training for such difficulties. To give two examples: Getting up in the night after only a few hours of sleep and going for a run in a tired state can be good mental preparation for an ultra race (and also helps to get some headlamp hours in). Another such mind game is to carry out a long run so that you already pass by your destination before the end of the run. Having to head out again when already tired helps to get the mind into a state that is extremely beneficial (if not even mandatory) for ultra runners: You just run. Whenever you get the thought of discontinuing for reasons other than a clear medical sign like an injury, you tell yourself that this is not a decision you want to make during a race - after the race, you can still evaluate if you're going to do something like that again (and in many cases, the answer is yes).

Now to the specific planning of the training. After already having defined the general focus of the intensity, namely the Power that equals $IF_{max} \cdot FTP$, the other important input to be determined is the training load. As a general recommendation which is also consistently applied here, the maximum training load should be reached around four weeks before the race. For an 8-week preparation, this corresponds to week 4, and for a 12-week preparation to week 8 of the plan. The minimum of the total training load in this peak week should at least reach the expected training load of the race itself. However, depending on the training level, the optimal value can be considerably higher for short and medium races. Let us have a closer look at what this means. At first, it is necessary to calculate the expected TSS of the race, which is the Power-based quantity that refers to the training load of a workout as introduced in Section 3.3. Using the corresponding definition, it is calculated as

$$TSS_{est,race} = \left(IF_{max}\right)^2 \cdot t_{est,race} \cdot 100.$$

We are going to illustrate this again with a few examples, which are listed in Table 5.1. The first case is a race with an estimated duration of 2 hours, leading to a quite high possible intensity factor of 0.91. This implies an anticipated TSS of 165, which, when divided by 7, gives a target ATL of 24 for the peak week. Such a training load is reachable even with a low training volume before the preparatory phase,

Example Number	$t_{est,race}$	IF_{max}	$TSS_{est,race}$	ATL (peak week, TSS/day)
1	2 h	0.96	185	26
2	8 h 30 min (8.5 h)	0.74	470	67
3	20 h	0.66	873	125

Table 5.1: Race examples of different duration with their estimated TSS, defining the minimum acute training load ATL in the peak week.

making such a race also feasible for newcomers. The situation is already entirely different for the second example, where the expected duration of 8 h 30 min together with the resulting target IF leads to a race TSS of 470. The minimum peak-week ATL_{peak} of 67 already requires quite some dedication. When calculating with one rest day in this week and using IF_{max} as an average reference, reaching the minimum goal for the training load still requires almost 1 h 30 min of average training duration for the other six days. This is even more extreme in the case of the third example race, an ultra run with an expected duration of around 20 h. Reaching the corresponding ATL_{peak} goal of 125 becomes quite a challenge - applying the same calculation as for the second example leads to an average duration of more than 3 h for the six training days of that week.

Calculating the minimum required ATL for the week of maximum training from the expected race TSS brings us a large step closer to setting up a training plan. However, we are not quite there yet; there are still two points to be discussed. Let us go back to example race 1. As already stated, the minimum ATL_{peak} requirement is relatively low in this case. It might be a suitable goal for beginners, but it is far too low for a well-trained athlete and could even lead to detraining in this case. To which value should it be raised then? The answer to this question depends on the training situation at the beginning of the preparation, where the CTL_{init} at that time is a relevant key factor. In case the phase before was comparably relaxed and did not involve any other dedicated preparation, a suitable target peak ATL could be 1.6 times the one of CTL_{init} for an 8-week plan and 1.8 times CTL_{init} in case of a 12-week schedule. However, this is just a rough suggestion. Of course the final choice is up to the runner, who should particularly keep in mind the danger of a too fast increase of the training load. An additional factor that can help with the decision is the training history. If higher ATL values during the preparation to similar races were handled without problems in the past, these might serve as a good reference for ATL_{peak}. In the situation that the runner just finished another race and corresponding dedicated preparation, a potential further rise of the training load should be properly thought through. Setting the ATL_{peak} goal to 1.3 of CTL_{init} would ensure that the runner can still recover from the past race at the beginning of the plan and end up with a CTL at the target race that is similar to the initial one.

If you plan to run a longer race, such as the one from the third example, the chances are high that you do not want to increase the minimum ATL_{peak} value (125 for the example). In this case, the relevant question is rather how large CTL_{init} should be, i.e., with which average training load should be started into the plan such that it does not lead to overstressing. An approximate reference value for an 8-week plan is between $CTL_{init} \approx ATL_{peak}/1.4$ and $ATL_{peak}/1.8$, corresponding to 89 respectively 69 for the example. The longer preparation time of the 12-week plan allows starting with a lower initial CTL_{init}, where a value in the range of $ATL_{peak}/1.6$ and $ATL_{peak}/2.0$ should be a good choice. For example 3, this yields a range of 63-78.

Once an appropriate value for ATL_{peak} has been determined, it can be used together with IF_{max} to set up a training plan. The dedicated description can be found together with two examples in Sections 6.2 to 6.4. In the following, we'll assume that you have adequately prepared for the race and now develop a strategy for this important day.

5.3 RACE STRATEGY

When the race is getting closer, it is time to develop a strategy for it. Already weeks ago, you estimated what finishing time is realistic, calculated the corresponding intensity IF_{max}, and have now hopefully prepared yourself properly to hold this intensity for the required time. Now the question is how to ration the available resources most efficiently.

Fortunately, there is a clear and universally valid answer in this case which, summarised in one word, is: Uniformity. Regardless of the duration, holding the target Power level steadily throughout the race is generally known to deliver optimal results. The reason behind this is that variation causes additional muscular exhaustion and also requires the body to adjust the energy supply and other relevant processes. Viewed from a different perspective, the target intensity IF_{max} for the race is by definition based on the normalized Power, which is higher than the average Power as it takes variations into account (see Section 3.3). However, the duration that is needed to finish the race depends on the average Power. It is therefore essential to keep variations at a minimum such that the average is as close as possible to the normalized Power. All your preparation before as well as your form on that day determine the normalized Power achievable for you in the race. Now it is up to you to maximize that potential by keeping the gap between average and normalized Power as small as feasible!

When following this concept of uniformity, it is straightforward to define a race strategy for road races. Just aim for a target Power of $P_{target} = IF_{max} \cdot FTP$ in this case and try to keep variations at a minimum. If you are still feeling good after around half of the race, it might be even worth considering raising the target slightly but only by a few percent. Of course, you can reevaluate any time after that, but you should generally refrain from raising the Power level before having finished the first half. Starting off too quickly is something that you would very likely regret later on.

When it comes to trail races, the situation gets a bit more complicated. Although the general goal of trying to lower variations to have average and normalized Power not far apart from each other is still valid, complete uniformity is usually utopistic here. Technical sections and descents make it harder or even dangerous to maintain a prescribed Power level. A suggested approach that should generally be applicable is the following:

- First, calculate the overall target Power as given above, i.e., via $P_{target} = IF_{max} \cdot FTP$. In the case of a 10-hour race and an FTP of 332 W it would be

$P_{target} = 0.73 \cdot 332 \, W = 243 \, W$.

- Define a general Power goal for all uphill sections. This can be set a bit higher than the overall target Power - by how much depends on the altitude profile, but a value of around 5% should usually be a good choice. For a route with a high level of ascents and descents, it can be increased to 10%, which should be considered an upper limit - using 5% for our example race results in

$P_{target,up} = 243 \, W \cdot 1.05 = 255 \, W$.

- The goal for flat, non-technical sections is the nominal target Power P_{target}.

- When running downhill, avoid looking at the Power display and just run according to your feeling. The Power level should automatically drop in most cases, by how much depends on the slope.

- As for technical sections, also try to check the Power level only sparsely and when safely possible. Avoid forcing to reach the target Power by any means and try to run comfortably. However, if you are noticing that you are overreaching, try to lower the intensity.

In addition to these recommendations, some races/routes with narrow sections might require running at a higher Power right at the beginning. Since most competitors will start off too quickly, it can be a good strategic decision to also begin at a higher Power level for those races. After all, even a perfect strategy won't help you that much if 15 minutes after the start you are on a path where you cannot overtake runners who are actually slower than you but started way too quickly for their performance level. In that case, also starting off faster can pay off, but always keep in mind that this comes at a price. There is absolutely no chance that you can run several hours at or above your FTP on race day by some miracle, even if your adrenaline level might give you another impression at the beginning. It is thus wise to limit this measure, both in terms of intensity and duration.

The presented approach of developing a race strategy based on the expected duration and the runner's FTP has already been successfully applied, where one example is

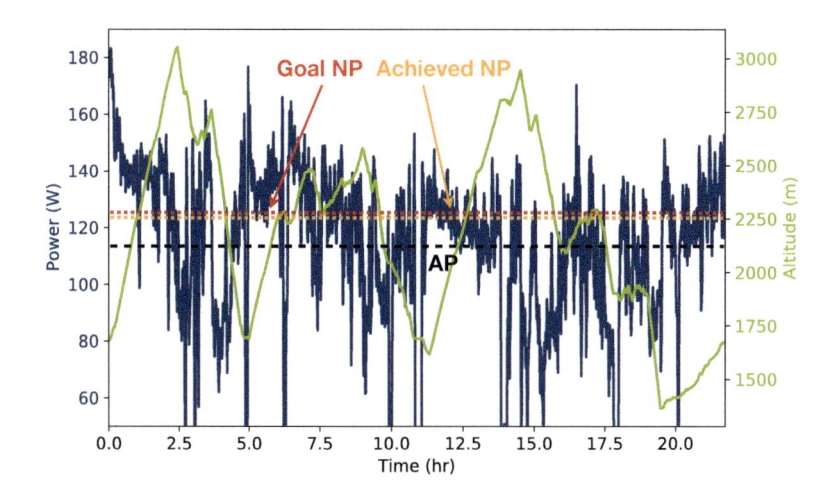

Figure 5.4: Power chart and altitude profile of an ultra-trail race conducted following the approach described here. Dips of the Power below the bottom of the figure mostly correspond to food stations.

shown in Figure 5.4. The route is a very technical trail located in mostly high-alpine terrain and includes the crossing of a glacier as well as the traversing of numerous fields of massive rocks. The above-described strategy was adopted according to the description, including a higher Power level at the beginning because of an upcoming narrow course section, which was quickly lowered after that. Following the strategy paid off, which is visible by the fact that the target Power could even be held for a longer time after more than 20 hours until the end of the race. This is also apparent from the TIF value of 0.98, proving that IF_{max} was correctly estimated.

5.4 ON RACE DAY

Finally, your race day has come. You have probably waited and prepared long for this, and now is the time to (hopefully) realize your goals. Make sure to eat and sleep well the days before and lower your ATL according to the plan. The purpose of all this is to bring you in the best possible shape to face the challenge and reach or maybe even surpass your expectations.

To ensure a proper Power calculation, add the weight of your backpack in the corresponding settings. Here it is worth considering not to add the full weight but to subtract a bit to account for the fact that the average weight of the backpack will be lower once you start to drink. Moreover, make sure that potential other Power meter settings are how you'd like them during the race, especially the averaging time. And most importantly, memorize your target Power level(s), maybe even consider writing them on your hand.

Once you are out in the race, follow your strategy and always keep in mind that uniformity is key. This does not mean that you should check your Power level every 5 seconds. Just have a look from time to time and use it to calibrate your perceived effort. Keep in mind that the Power meter can sometimes err, but if the values are consistently higher than you expect them to be at the beginning, the chances are high that your own perception is wrong. If you are still feeling good in the middle of the race, you can consider raising the target Power. However, if you have problems holding the level and are not feeling well, don't despair. There are many factors that influence your daily form, and it is impossible to control all of them. Just listen to your body and try to make the best out of it. Good luck and all the best!

5.5 SUMMARY

The following list gives a quick-look overview of the concepts introduced in this chapter:

1. Estimate the time it takes you to finish the race ($t_{est,race}$), using the methods discussed in Section 5.1. Ideally to be done two to three months before the race.

2. Calculate the target intensity factor IF_{max} from $t_{est,race}$, for example using Figure 5.3.

3. Use IF_{max} and $t_{est,race}$ to calculate the estimated race training load via $TSS_{est,race} = IF_{max}^2 \cdot t_{est,race} \cdot 100$.

4. $TSS_{est,race}/7$ corresponds to the minimum value of ATL_{peak}, but it might have to be scaled up depending on the race duration and your training level. For long races, in turn, you should make sure that your CTL at the beginning of the race preparation phase is not too low.

5. Use IF_{max} and ATL_{peak} to generate a training plan as described in Section 6.2.

6. Racing: Try to run with a uniform Power output. The reference target Power is $P_{target} = IF_{max} \cdot FTP$. For road races, try to hold this value. For trail and mountain races, aim for a slightly (typically 5%) higher Power on the ascents, for the nominal one on flat sections, and try to run according to your feeling on technical and downhill sections. Incorporate narrow sections at the beginning in your planning. After around half of the race, you can think about raising the target Power level a bit but avoid major upward adjustments before.

6 - WORKOUTS AND TRAINING PLANS

This concluding chapter contains a selection of workouts, followed by a description of how to define a training plan for a specific race using the relevant custom input obtained in Section 5.2. That method is finally applied to two schematic race examples.

6.1 KEY WORKOUTS

In the following, some specific workouts that are both fun and efficient for your training are going to be highlighted. Whether you are creating a training plan or just looking for some variety in your training, this small collection hopefully has something for you. If you are training on trails or mountainous terrain, make sure to plan the route such that technical or downhill sections coincide with workout parts at a lower intensity. Never enforce a higher Power when it brings an increased risk of injuries! Additionally, always keep in mind that you do not have to reach the Power goal of a given section from the first second on. This is especially important at the beginning of a workout when your body still has to warm up. Even though warm-up phases are generally included in the workout descriptions, make sure to start running slowly at the very beginning. Then ramp up the Power within the first minute until you have reached the nominal warm-up Power. Regarding the settings of your Power meter, make sure to use a shorter averaging time (e.g., 10 seconds) for all workouts where the target Power is often changed.

Many of the workouts in this section are admittedly quite intense. Only consider carrying them out when you are in the physical condition to do so (as, e.g., attested by a doctor), and avoid trying to stick to a given intensity at all costs when it doesn't appear feasible or healthy. In other words, these workouts are just suggestions which you conduct at your own risk. Furthermore, the "bread and butter" of your training should consist of runs at moderate Power. This is why we will begin with a very simple yet essential workout.

The Boring One

This workout corresponds to an easy run at moderate but constant intensity (see overview figure). Just try to roughly

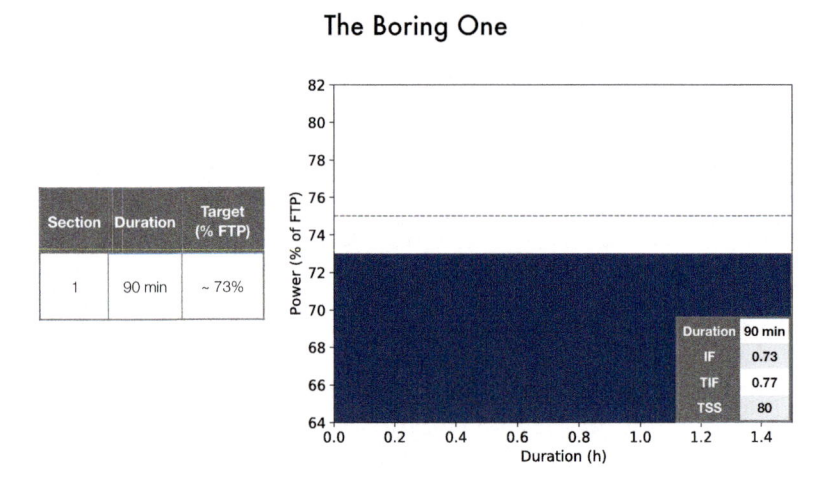

The Boring One

Section	Duration	Target (% FTP)
1	90 min	~ 73%

Duration	90 min
IF	0.73
TIF	0.77
TSS	80

hold the target Power (i.e., the given percentage multiplied with your FTP value) steadily the entire time whenever the terrain allows it. Of course, feel free to carry out this workout at a different intensity (ideally not too high) or duration. The TSS in case of such a modification is for this workout easily given as $\left(\dfrac{P_{\text{target}}}{\text{FTP}}\right)^2 \cdot t \cdot 100$, where t corresponds to the time in units of hours.

Sweet-Spot Training (SST)

This type of training is a very effective way to accustom your body to higher overall intensities, which is not only beneficial for those targeting short or medium distances but also for ultra runners. The aim is to stay at a Power level that challenges the body but can still be adequately held for a longer time during the training. Here two different ver-

SST - Shorter Version

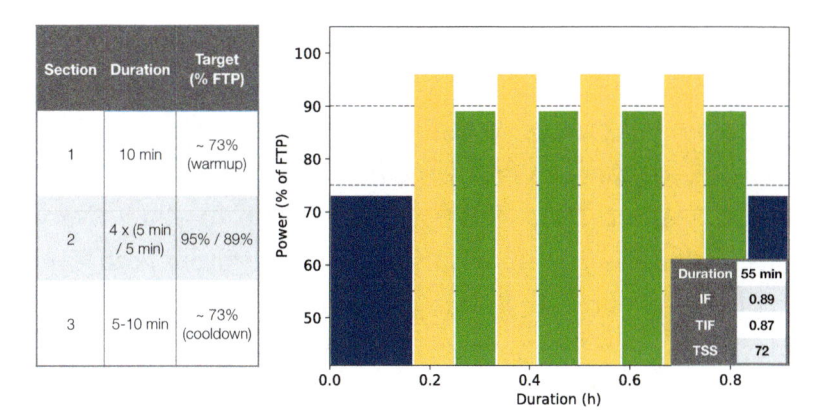

Section	Duration	Target (% FTP)
1	10 min	~ 73% (warmup)
2	4 x (5 min / 5 min)	95% / 89%
3	5-10 min	~ 73% (cooldown)

Duration	55 min
IF	0.89
TIF	0.87
TSS	72

sions are presented: A shorter one with one high-intensity block of 40 minutes duration and a longer one consisting of two 30-minute blocks with some rest in between. When running in the mountains, this recovery section can be chosen such that it corresponds to a downhill part. Especially the longer workout is quite intense, which should be considered in the overall planning of the preceding and subsequent training sessions.

SST - Longer Version

Section	Duration	Target (% FTP)
1	10 min	~ 73% (warmup)
2	3 x (5 min / 5 min)	94% / 85%
3	5-10 min	50-70%
4	3 x (5 min / 5 min)	94% / 85%
5	5-10 min	~ 73% (cooldown)

Duration	80 min
IF	0.86
TIF	0.9
TSS	100

Threshold Run (2 x 15 min)

This workout trains you to get used to running at the FTP level, which can also greatly help to increase it. The 2 x 15 minutes are just a suggestion, and it's up to you to vary this, as long as you are ensuring enough recovery both during the workout as well as before and after it. If you are trying the training for the first time or just want an easier version of it, consider only doing the first of the two blocks and the recovery part, and then run the second block at a lower intensity, such as 75% or 80% FTP.

Threshold (2 x 15 min)

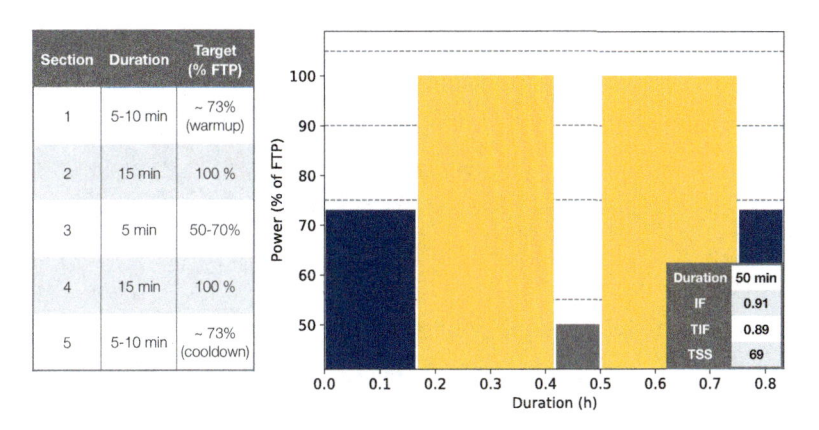

Section	Duration	Target (% FTP)
1	5-10 min	~ 73% (warmup)
2	15 min	100 %
3	5 min	50-70%
4	15 min	100 %
5	5-10 min	~ 73% (cooldown)

Duration	50 min
IF	0.91
TIF	0.89
TSS	69

8 x 3 min

This VO2$_{max}$-focused training consists of a set of intervals that are good for building up speed, making it especially well suited for the off-season. Try to consistently hit the high-intensity target goal right from the beginning - if you instead overshoot at the start, the chances are high that you will regret this later on. When you do this training for the first time, don't push yourself too hard. Be assured that already managing a few repetitions results in an efficient training stimulus.

8 × 3 min

Section	Duration	Target (% FTP)
1	10 min	~ 73% (warmup)
2	8 x (3 min / 2 min)	110% / 50%
3	5-10 min	~ 73% (cooldown)

Duration	55 min
IF	0.93
TIF	0.91
TSS	79

4 × 8 min

Although the concept is similar to the 8 x 3 min intervals, holding a target Power that is even slightly above your FTP value repeatedly for 8 minutes is really challenging. However, nobody said that getting faster comes without effort, and

4 × 8 min

Section	Duration	Target (% FTP)
1	10 min	~ 73% (warmup)
2	4 x (8 min / 4 min)	103% / 50%
3	5-10 min	~ 73% (cooldown)

Duration	63 min
IF	0.90
TIF	0.91
TSS	85

once you've done this workout (or at least part of it), you may get the feeling that this was an effective way towards that goal.

1 min / 1 min

Consider this an alternative to the 8 x 3 min workout for clocking in some $VO2_{max}$ time. Switching between 110% and 60% FTP every minute ensures that you always get rest when you start to need it, and therefore you'll spend quite some time in the $VO2_{max}$ Power zone.

1 min / 1 min

Section	Duration	Target (% FTP)
1	10 min	~ 73% (warmup)
2	12 x (1 min / 1 min)	110% / 60%
3	2 min	60 %
4	12 x (1 min / 1 min)	110% / 60%
5	5-10 min	~ 73% (cooldown)

Duration	65 min
IF	0.90
TIF	0.91
TSS	88

High-Intensity Variation

The target zones and times are probably hard to remember for this workout, so it is best saved and conducted with the targets displayed on the watch. The high-intensity phases that are followed by five minutes in the Tempo zone are

High-Intensity Variation

Section	Duration	Target (% FTP)
warm-up	5 min	~ 73% (warmup)
(green)	5 min	81 %
(grey)	1 min	50 %
(orange)	2 min	115 %
(red)	1 min	125 %
cooldown	5 min	~ 60%

Duration: 64 min; IF: 0.88; TIF: 0.89; TSS: 83

quite demanding. The subsequent one-minute recovery helps a bit, but expect it to be challenging!

Moderate Tempo

This one is conceptually very similar to an SST workout, but especially the lower-intensity parts are more moderate.

Moderate Tempo

Section	Duration	Target (% FTP)
1	10 min	~ 73% (warmup)
2	5 x (5 min / 5 min)	90% / 75%
3	5 min	~ 70% (cooldown)

Duration: 65 min; IF: 0.81; TIF: 0.82; TSS: 72

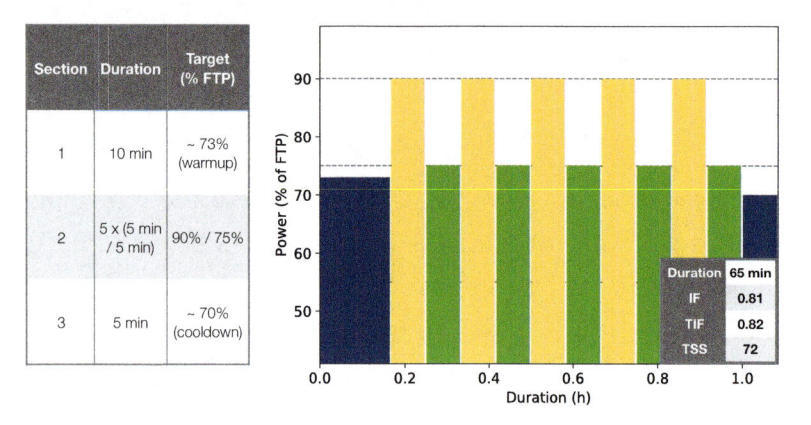

118

It is therefore well suited for days where you want to do a tempo session without exaggerating, or generally when you want to get used to higher Power zones.

3 x 20 min

The combination of a high fraction in the Tempo zone and the overall duration make this training demanding and requires a well-developed base endurance. It is ideally suited for training uphill running or speed hiking, assuming you have a sufficiently high mountain nearby. Needless to say that sufficient recovery is obligatory. If you are very well trained, you can even consider adding a fourth block.

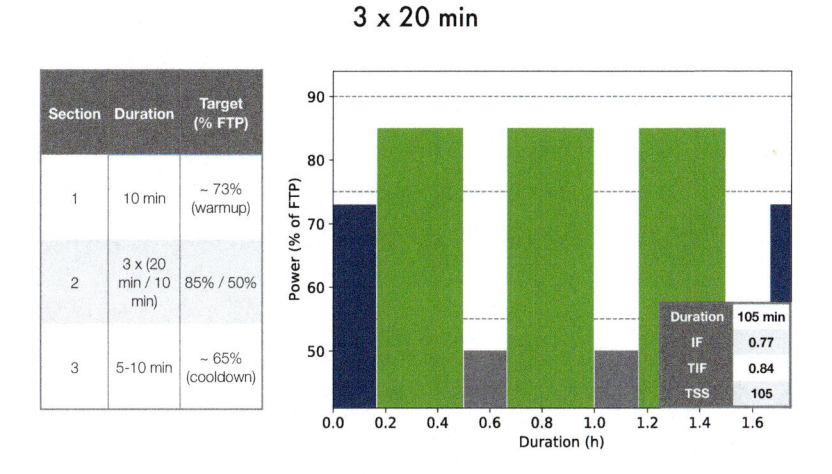

3 x 20 min

Section	Duration	Target (% FTP)
1	10 min	~ 73% (warmup)
2	3 x (20 min / 10 min)	85% / 50%
3	5-10 min	~ 65% (cooldown)

Duration	105 min
IF	0.77
TIF	0.84
TSS	105

Long Run with Variation

While traditional long runs at constant intensity are already suitable for improving base endurance, this alternative is an excellent way of preparing for ultra races (see the ex-

Long Run with Variation

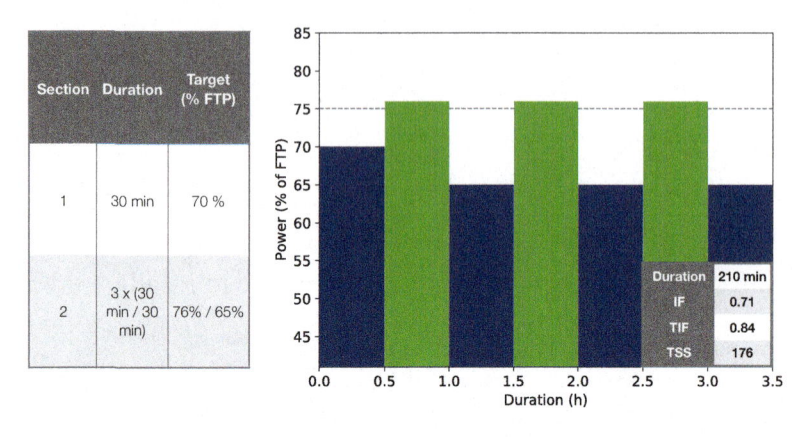

Section	Duration	Target (% FTP)
1	30 min	70 %
2	3 x (30 min / 30 min)	76% / 65%

Duration	210 min
IF	0.71
TIF	0.84
TSS	176

planation in Section 5.2). In the presented way, the workout consists of blocks with a duration of 30 minutes each. The high-intensity sections are run at race target Power, which in this case (76%) corresponds to a race with an expected duration of 7 hours. If you are preparing for a shorter race and the target Power is correspondingly higher, you might have to consider shortening these more intense sections. The same should be considered when you want to extend the overall duration of the workout.

6.2 SETTING UP A TRAINING PLAN

Finally, let us discuss how to set up a plan to train for a specific race. Of course, you don't need an actual race for generating such a schedule but can also prepare for a fictive one, such as a shorter one in the off-season to improve your overall speed. As already discussed in Section 5.2, the following input is needed to proceed:

- The duration of the training plan - 8 or 12 weeks.
- Your initial chronic training load (CTL_{init}) at the beginning of the plan. It corresponds to the amount of training stress your body is currently used to.
- The classification of your recent load with respect to your training history. Was this period a relatively relaxed one or already quite challenging? The answer to this question determines by how much the load can be increased in the upcoming weeks. The recommended range for the acute training load in the peak week is $ATL_{peak} = (1.3 - 2.0) \cdot CTL_{init}$ in the case of an 8-week plan and $ATL_{peak} = (1.3 - 2.2) \cdot CTL_{init}$ for a 12-week schedule.
- The minimum value for ATL_{peak} is given by the expected training load of the race ($TSS_{est,race}$), such that $ATL_{peak} = TSS_{est,race}/7$. For ultra races, this criterion should be considered already before the race-specific preparation to ensure that CTL_{init} is not too low.

Based on the duration, CTL_{init}, and ATL_{peak}, the training load for the different upcoming weeks is set. It is shown together with the corresponding evolution of ATL and CTL for the 8- and 12-week schedules in Figures 6.1 and 6.2, respectively. The respective tables contain the weekly targets for the ref-

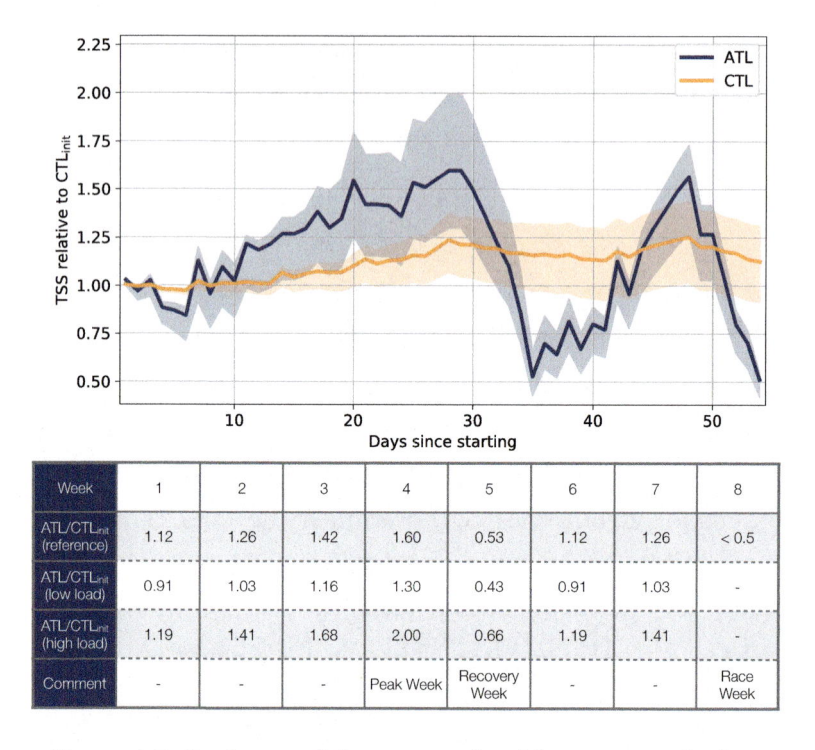

Week	1	2	3	4	5	6	7	8
ATL/CTL$_{init}$ (reference)	1.12	1.26	1.42	1.60	0.53	1.12	1.26	< 0.5
ATL/CTL$_{init}$ (low load)	0.91	1.03	1.16	1.30	0.43	0.91	1.03	-
ATL/CTL$_{init}$ (high load)	1.19	1.41	1.68	2.00	0.66	1.19	1.41	-
Comment	-	-	-	Peak Week	Recovery Week	-	-	Race Week

Figure 6.1: Evolution of the training load for an 8-week plan. The graph at the top shows the development of both ATL and CTL relative to CTL$_{init}$. The table below gives the target ATL/CTL$_{init}$ values for each week.

erence values of ATL$_{peak}$/CTL$_{init}$ (i.e., 1.6 for 8 weeks and 1.8 for 12 weeks), as well as the ones for lower and higher load. For both training plan durations, the load is gradually increased during the first four weeks, where the fourth week corresponds to the overall training peak in the case of the 8-week preparation. The goal of the fifth week is to rest in order to recover from the previous strain. As for the 8-week

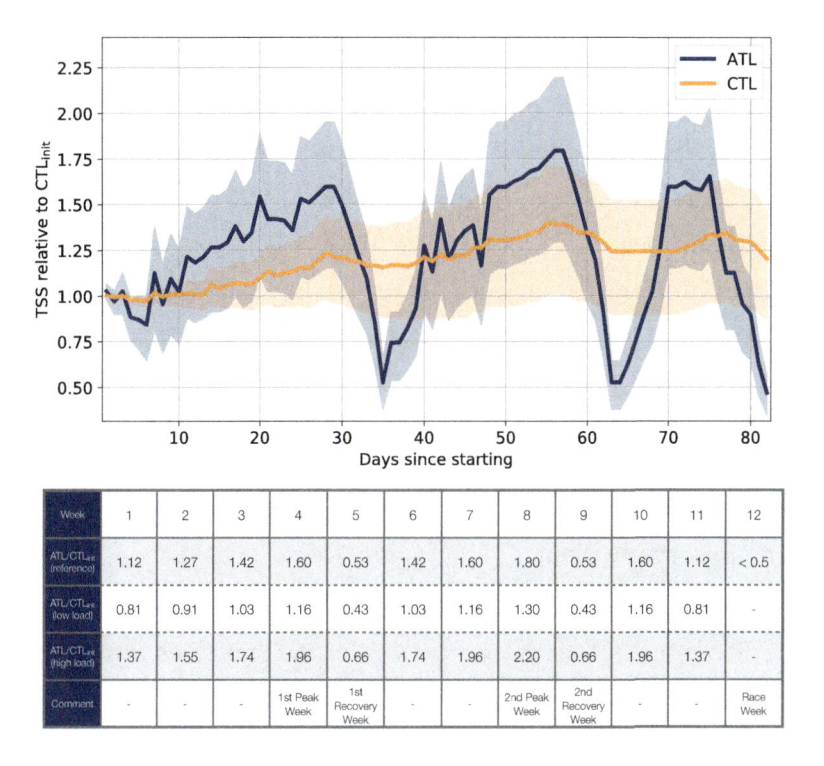

Figure 6.2: Evolution of the training load for a 12-week training plan.

plan, weeks 6 and 7 are again similar to weeks 1 and 2, followed by the race week with a much lower load to overcompensate and be in the best shape for the race. In the case of the 12-week plan, the weeks 6 to 8 are more challenging, where the eighth week corresponds to the one with the overall highest load. Following that, week 9 should again be used for recovery, followed by the last intense week 10. After that, the ATL has to be considerably reduced not to carry residual fatigue into the race.

Once the ATL/CTL$_{init}$ goal for each week has been determined, the total weekly TSS budget is calculated by multiplying the values with CTL$_{init}$ · 7. For example, a target value of ATL/CTL$_{init}$ = 1.42 together with CTL$_{init}$ = 50 yields an overall TSS of 1.42 · 50 · 7 = 497, which is to be distributed over that week. After having calculated the corresponding load for each week, the final remaining question is how and with which workouts the schedule should be filled to reasonably prepare you for the race. Again, there is not one perfect generalized way to do that. Nevertheless, with the following guidelines you should be able to set up an appropriate plan:

- **Your training should generally revolve around the intended target Power of the race.** This does not mean that the intensity factors of your training should all be equal to your intended race IF. Your body certainly profits from also getting used to both lower and higher Power levels, but always keep in mind that the race target Power is where you want to perform most of the effort in the end.

- Plan in **at least one rest day per week**, in recovery weeks usually more.

- **Long runs:** This type of workout is not only relevant for ultra runners. Runs with a duration of at least two hours are beneficial in many different ways and should ideally be done at least once per week - how often and how long depends on the duration of your intended race.

But even if you are, e.g., focusing on one-hour races, your base endurance profits considerably from the occasional long run.

- More intense workouts: Even as an ultra runner, don't entirely rely on long and easy runs. Incorporating tempo sessions from time to time is not only efficient but also fun.

- Consider replacing some of the easy workouts with suitable alternative sports such as cycling or hiking. The heart-rate-based TSS estimation outlined in Section 4.2 can help to avoid data holes in your training logbook.

- Be creative: The workouts shown here, both in the previous section as well as the ones described in the example training plans, can help you in setting up a schedule. However, don't be shy to try out your own ideas as well!

- Consider re-assessing your FTP around the middle of the plan. To avoid overtraining, an FTP test can usually be fit into a recovery week, but not the tapering phase before the race!

- If injuries are bothering you, it is advisable to switch even more to alternative sports or reduce the training load. If that doesn't help, go visit a doctor.

In the following, two examples of training plans that were generated with the introduced scheme are presented.

6.3 EXAMPLE TRAINING PLAN - 8 WEEKS PREPARATION AND 3.5 H RACE DURATION

The first example plan was generated for a race-specific preparation of 8 weeks and an expected race duration of 3.5 hours. This duration yields $IF_{max} = 0.84$ (using the more conservative IF_{max} calculation for longer races) and an estimated race TSS of 247. This leads to a rather low corresponding $ATL_{peak,min}$ (TSS of 35 per day). If this would indeed be set as the target, the athlete might, depending on the conditions, end up detraining and not reach the duration goal. Instead, we use the initial training load and scale it reasonably to obtain ATL_{peak}. The initial chronic load CTL_{init} shall be 50, indicating regular training. It is furthermore assumed that the athlete is used to this training volume. Under these circumstances, the reference scaling from Figure 6.1 can be used, which gives $ATL_{peak} = 1.6 \cdot CTL_{init} = 80$, the planned training load for the fourth training week. The goals for the other weeks are then calculated correspondingly using the values from the same table row. The evolution of ATL and CTL for this plan is shown in Figure 6.3.

The detailed breakdown of suggested workouts is given below. The combination and variation of workouts should provide a proper training stimulus to prepare for a race of that expected duration. This takes into account the evolution of the training load as well as the focus on the race tar-

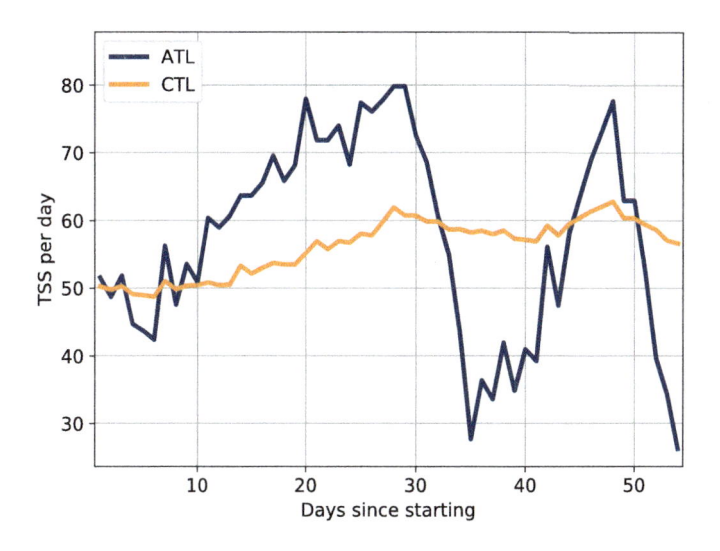

Figure 6.3: Evolution of ATL and CTL for the 8-week training plan example.

get Power. Of course, this merely covers the endurance part of the race preparation. Additional factors such as the type of terrain, altitude gain, etc., have to be included in the workout planning (see also the discussion in Section 5.2).

The workout list includes a short description, where quotation marks indicate references to workouts names from Section 6.1. Percentages correspond to Power levels with respect to the FTP, and "wu" and "cd" stand for warm-up and cooldown phases, respectively. In addition to this description, the TSS, IF, TIF, and workout duration are additionally provided.

Breakdown of suggested workouts for the 8-week training plan.

Week 1	Description	TSS	IF	TIF	Duration
Mon	10 min wu @73% 40 min @84% 5 min cd @73%	61	0.81	0.80	55 min
Tue	35 min @70% running, alternatively 50 min @60% biking	29 / 30	0.7 / 0.6	0.65 / 0.59	35 / 45 min
Wed	"Moderate Tempo" Workout	72	0.81	0.82	65 min
Thu	Rest Day	-	-	-	-
Fri	10 min wu @73% 25 min @84% 5 min cd @73%	43	0.80	0.76	40 min
Sat	50 min @70% running, alternatively 65 min @60% biking	41 / 39	0.7 / 0.6	0.68 / 0.61	50 min / 65 min
Sun	3 h @70% (long run)	147	0.7	0.81	180 min

Week 2	Description	TSS	IF	TIF	Duration
Mon	Rest Day	-	-	-	-
Tue	"SST - Shorter Version"	72	0.89	0.87	55 min
Wed	"The Boring One" (60 min)	53	0.73	0.73	60 min
Thu	10 min wu @73% 45 min @84% 5 min cd @73%	67	0.82	0.82	60 min
Fri	40 min @70% running, alternatively 55 min @60% biking	33	0.7 / 0.6	0.66 / 0.59	40 min / 55 min
Sat	"The Boring One" (60 min)	53	0.73	0.73	60 min
Sun	10 min wu @70% 3 x (20 min @84% + 40 min @65%)	168	0.73	0.86	190 min

Week 3	Description	TSS	IF	TIF	Duration
Mon	Rest Day	-	-	-	-
Tue	"4 x 8 min"	85	0.90	0.91	63 min
Wed	10 min wu @70% 2 x (20 min @84% + 15 min @70%)	81	0.78	0.81	80 min
Thu	50 min @70% running, alternatively 65 min @60% biking	41 / 39	0.7 / 0.6	0.68 / 0.61	50 min / 65 min
Fri	10 min wu @73% 30 min @84% 5 min cd @73%	49	0.81	0.78	45 min
Sat	2 h 30 min @70% (long run)	122	0.7	0.79	150 min
Sun	10 min wu @70% 3 x (20 min @84% + 20 min @65%)	125	0.76	0.84	130 min

Week 4	Description	TSS	IF	TIF	Duration
Mon	Rest Day	-	-	-	-
Tue	"SST - Longer Version"	100	0.86	0.9	80 min
Wed	50 min @70% running, alternatively 65 min @60% biking	41 / 39	0.7 / 0.6	0.68 / 0.61	50 min / 65 min
Thu	"3 x 20 min"	105	0.77	0.84	105 min
Fri	"The Boring One" (45 min)	40	0.73	0.70	45 min
Sat	10 min wu @73% 3 x (20 min @84% + 20 min @73%)	134	0.79	0.88	130 min
Sun	140 min @70% 20 min @84%	139	0.72	0.83	160 min

Week 5	Description	TSS	IF	TIF	Duration
Mon	Rest Day	-	-	-	-
Tue	10 min wu @73% 30 min @84% 5 min cd @73%	49	0.81	0.78	45 min
Wed	30 min @50% biking	13	0.5	0.45	30 min
Thu	10 min wu @73% 20 min @102% FTP test 5 min cd @73%	50	0.93	0.86	35 min
Fri	Rest Day	-	-	-	-
Sat	"The Boring One" (60 min)	53	0.73	0.73	60 min
Sun	35 min @70% running, alternatively 50 min @60% biking	29 / 30	0.7 / 0.6	0.65 / 0.59	35 / 45 min

Week 6	Description	TSS	IF	TIF	Duration
Mon	10 min wu @73% 40 min @84% 5 min cd @73%	61	0.81	0.80	55 min
Tue	35 min @70% running, alternatively 50 min @60% biking	29 / 30	0.7 / 0.6	0.65 / 0.59	35 / 45 min
Wed	"Moderate Tempo" Workout	72	0.81	0.82	65 min
Thu	Rest Day	-	-	-	-
Fri	10 min wu @73% 25 min @84% 5 min cd @73%	43	0.80	0.76	40 min
Sat	50 min @70% running, alternatively 65 min @60% biking	41 / 39	0.7 / 0.6	0.68 / 0.61	50 min / 65 min
Sun	3 h @70% (long run)	147	0.7	0.81	180 min

Week 7	Description	TSS	IF	TIF	Duration
Mon	Rest Day	-	-	-	-
Tue	"3 x 20 min"	105	0.77	0.84	105 min
Wed	80 min @75% 30 min @84%	111	0.78	0.85	110 min
Thu	45 min @70% running, alternatively 60 min @60% biking	37 / 36	0.7 / 0.6	0.67 / 0.6	45 min / 60 min
Fri	"SST - Shorter Version"	72	0.89	0.87	55 min
Sat	"Moderate Tempo" Workout	72	0.81	0.82	65 min
Sun	"The Boring One" (50 min)	44	0.73	0.71	50 min

Week 8	Description	TSS	IF	TIF	Duration
Mon	Rest Day	-	-	-	-
Tue	10 min wu @73% 15 min @84% 5 min cd @73%	31	0.79	0.72	30 min
Wed	"The Boring One" (25 min)	22	0.73	0.65	25 min
Thu	Rest Day	-	-	-	-
Fri	5 min wu @73% 5 min @84% 5 min cd @73%	15	0.77	0.64	15 min
Sat	**Race**	**247**	**0.84**	**1.00**	**210 min**

6.4 EXAMPLE TRAINING PLAN - 12 WEEKS PREPARATION AND 10 H RACE DURATION

The second example of a training plan shows how to prepare for an ultra race with an expected duration of 10 hours and for an extended preparation phase of 12 weeks. In this case, $IF_{max} = 0.73$, and the expected TSS of the race is 529, which gives $ATL_{peak,min} = 76$. For a 12-week preparation and the corresponding reference scaling of $ATL_{peak} = 1.8 \cdot CTL_{init}$, the minimum initial chronic load

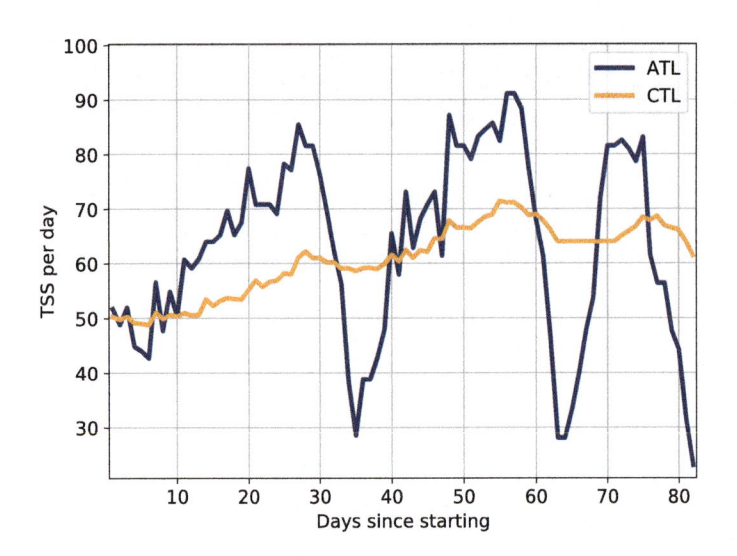

Figure 6.4: Evolution of ATL and CTL for the presented 12-week plan.

is $CTL_{init} = 42$, respectively 38 in case of a more aggressive increase of $ATL_{peak} = 2.0 \cdot CTL_{init}$. However, the presented plan again assumes $CTL_{init} = 50$ and uses the reference scaling (1.8), which leads to $ATL_{peak} = 1.8 \cdot 50 = 90$. The plan's overall progression of ATL and CTL is shown in Figure 6.4, following the general scheme introduced in Section 6.2. Owing to the lower race target Power, the plan contains fewer high-intensity workouts, which, together with the higher value of ATL_{peak}, implies a higher number of training hours compared to the other presented schedule. Assuming that the race duration was estimated correctly and the CTL_{init} value is representative of the all-season training load of the runner, this plan should adequately prepare the runner for a successful race.

Breakdown of suggested workouts for the 12-week training plan.

Week 1	Description	TSS	IF	TIF	Duration
Mon	"The Boring One" (70 min)	62	0.73	0.75	70 min
Tue	35 min @70% running, alternatively 50 min @60% biking	29 / 30	0.7 / 0.6	0.65 / 0.59	35 / 45 min
Wed	"Moderate Tempo" Workout	72	0.81	0.82	65 min
Thu	Rest Day	-	-	-	-
Fri	2 x (10 min @70% + 10 min @ 76%) 10 min @70%	44	0.73	0.71	50 min
Sat	50 min @70% running, alternatively 65 min @60% biking	41 / 39	0.7 / 0.6	0.68 / 0.61	50 min / 65 min
Sun	3 h @70% (long run)	147	0.7	0.81	180 min

Week 2	Description	TSS	IF	TIF	Duration
Mon	Rest Day	-	-	-	-
Tue	"The Boring One" (90 min)	80	0.73	0.77	90 min
Wed	50 min @70% running, alternatively 65 min @60% biking	41 / 39	0.7 / 0.6	0.68 / 0.61	50 min / 65 min
Thu	"Moderate Tempo" Workout	72	0.81	0.82	65 min
Fri	40 min @70% running, alternatively 55 min @60% biking	33	0.7 / 0.6	0.66 / 0.59	40 min / 55 min
Sat	"The Boring One" (60 min)	53	0.73	0.73	60 min
Sun	30 min @70% 3 x (30 min @73% + 30 min @65%)	169	0.69	0.83	210 min

Week 3	Description	TSS	IF	TIF	Duration
Mon	Rest Day	-	-	-	-
Tue	"The Boring One" (100 min)	89	0.73	0.78	100 min
Wed	"Moderate Tempo" Workout	72	0.81	0.82	65 min
Thu	50 min @70% running, alternatively 65 min @60% biking	41 / 39	0.7 / 0.6	0.68 / 0.61	50 min / 65 min
Fri	2 x (10 min @70% + 10 min @ 76%) 20 min @70%	52	0.72	0.72	60 min
Sat	2 h 30 min @70% (long run)	122	0.7	0.79	150 min
Sun	3 x (30 min @73% + 20 min @65%)	123	0.70	0.80	150 min

Week 4	Description	TSS	IF	TIF	Duration
Mon	Rest Day	-	-	-	-
Tue	"The Boring One" (100 min)	89	0.73	0.78	100 min
Wed	2 x (10 min @70% + 10 min @ 76%) 30 min @70%	60	0.72	0.73	70 min
Thu	"3 x 20 min"	105	0.77	0.84	105 min
Fri	50 min @70% running, alternatively 65 min @60% biking	41 / 39	0.7 / 0.6	0.68 / 0.61	50 min / 65 min
Sat	240 min @67%	180	0.67	0.81	240 min
Sun	30 min @70% 2 x (20 min @76% + 20 min @70%)	96	0.72	0.79	110 min

Week 5	Description	TSS	IF	TIF	Duration
Mon	Rest Day	-	-	-	-
Tue	2 x (10 min @70% + 10 min @ 76%) 20 min @70%	52	0.72	0.72	60 min
Wed	30 min @50% biking	13	0.5	0.45	30 min
Thu	"The Boring One" (60 min)	53	0.73	0.73	60 min
Fri	Rest Day	-	-	-	-
Sat	"The Boring One" (60 min)	53	0.73	0.73	60 min
Sun	35 min @70% running, alternatively 50 min @60% biking	29 / 30	0.7 / 0.6	0.65 / 0.59	35 / 45 min

Week 6	Description	TSS	IF	TIF	Duration
Mon	"Moderate Tempo" Workout	72	0.81	0.82	65 min
Tue	2 x (10 min @70% + 10 min @ 76%) 20 min @70%	52	0.72	0.72	60 min
Wed	50 min @70% running, alternatively 65 min @60% biking	41 / 39	0.7 / 0.6	0.68 / 0.61	50 min / 65 min
Thu	"The Boring One" (100 min)	89	0.73	0.78	100 min
Fri	3 x (30 min @73% + 20 min @65%)	123	0.70	0.80	150 min
Sat	Rest Day	-	-	-	-
Sun	3 h @67%	135	0.67	0.78	180 min

Week 7	Description	TSS	IF	TIF	Duration
Mon	Rest Day	-	-	-	-
Tue	"The Boring One" (100 min)	89	0.73	0.78	100 min
Wed	2 x (10 min @70% + 10 min @ 76%) 30 min @70%	60	0.72	0.73	70 min
Thu	"3 x 20 min"	105	0.77	0.84	105 min
Fri	50 min @70% running, alternatively 65 min @60% biking	41 / 39	0.7 / 0.6	0.68 / 0.61	50 min / 65 min
Sat	240 min @67%	180	0.67	0.81	240 min
Sun	30 min @70% 2 x (20 min @76% + 20 min @70%)	96	0.72	0.79	110 min

Week 8	Description	TSS	IF	TIF	Duration
Mon	Rest Day	-	-	-	-
Tue	"Moderate Tempo" Workout	72	0.81	0.82	65 min
Wed	"The Boring One" (100 min)	89	0.73	0.78	100 min
Thu	50 min @73% 20 min @85% 50 min @73%	114	0.75	0.83	120 min
Fri	60 min @70% running, alternatively 75 min @60% biking	49 / 45	0.7 / 0.6	0.70 / 0.62	60 min / 75 min
Sat	4 x (20 min @73% + 30 min @65%)	157	0.69	0.81	200 min
Sun	210 min @67%	157	0.67	0.80	210 min

Week 9	Description	TSS	IF	TIF	Duration
Mon	*Rest Day*	-	-	-	-
Tue	2 x (10 min @70% + 10 min @ 76%) 20 min @70%	52	0.72	0.72	60 min
Wed	30 min @50% biking	13	0.5	0.45	30 min
Thu	10 min wu @73% 20 min @102% FTP test 5 min cd @73%	50	0.93	0.86	35 min
Fri	*Rest Day*	-	-	-	-
Sat	"The Boring One" (60 min)	53	0.73	0.73	60 min
Sun	35 min @70% running, *alternatively* 50 min @60% biking	29 / 30	0.7 / 0.6	0.65 / 0.59	35 / 45 min

Week 10	Description	TSS	IF	TIF	Duration
Mon	*Rest Day*	-	-	-	-
Tue	"The Boring One" (100 min)	89	0.73	0.78	100 min
Wed	2 x (10 min @70% + 10 min @ 76%) 30 min @70%	60	0.72	0.73	70 min
Thu	"3 x 20 min"	105	0.77	0.84	105 min
Fri	50 min @70% running, *alternatively* 65 min @60% biking	41 / 39	0.7 / 0.6	0.68 / 0.61	50 min / 65 min
Sat	240 min @67%	180	0.67	0.81	240 min
Sun	30 min @70% 2 x (20 min @76% + 20 min @70%)	96	0.72	0.79	110 min

Week 11	Description	TSS	IF	TIF	Duration
Mon	*Rest Day*	-	-	-	-
Tue	30 min @70% 2 x (20 min @76% + 20 min @70%)	96	0.72	0.79	110 min
Wed	60 min @70% running, *alternatively* 75 min @60% biking	49 / 45	0.7 / 0.6	0.70 / 0.62	60 min / 75 min
Thu	"The Boring One" (100 min)	89	0.73	0.78	100 min
Fri	"Moderate Tempo" Workout	72	0.81	0.82	65 min
Sat	35 min @70% running, *alternatively* 50 min @60% biking	29 / 30	0.7 / 0.6	0.65 / 0.59	35 / 45 min
Sun	2 x (10 min @70% + 10 min @ 76%) 30 min @70%	60	0.72	0.73	70 min

Week 12	Description	TSS	IF	TIF	Duration
Mon	*Rest Day*	-	-	-	-
Tue	20 min @70% 20 min @ 76%	35	0.73	0.69	40 min
Wed	30 min @70% running, *alternatively* 40 min @60% biking	25 / 24	0.7 / 0.6	0.64 / 0.57	30 / 40 min
Thu	*Rest Day*	-	-	-	-
Fri	15 min @73%	13	0.73	0.60	15 min
Sat	**Race**	**533**	**0.73**	**1.00**	**600 min**

REFERENCES

1. Kristine L. Snyder, Rodger Kram, Jinger S. Gottschall: "The role of elastic energy storage and recovery in downhill and uphill running", Journal of Experimental Biology, 1 July 2012, 215 (13): 2283–2287. DOI: https://doi.org/10.1242/jeb.066332
2. Functional Threshold Power: https://www.trainingpeaks.com/learn/articles/what-is-threshold-power/
3. Jim Vance: "Run with Power: The Complete Guide to Power Meters for Running", VeloPress 2016
4. Jim Vance's Running Power Zones: https://www.velopress.com/jim-vances-running-power-zones/
5. Andrew Coggan's Power Zones: https://www.trainingpeaks.com/blog/power-training-levels/
6. Normalized Power: https://www.trainingpeaks.com/blog/what-is-normalized-power/
7. IF, NP, TSS: https://www.trainingpeaks.com/learn/articles/normalized-power-intensity-factor-training-stress/
8. Strava GAP: https://support.strava.com/hc/en-us/articles/216917067-Grade-Adjusted-Pace-GAP-
9. About improving the strava GAP: https://medium.com/strava-engineering/an-improved-gap-model-8b07ae8886c3

10. Minetti, A. E. et al. (2002). Energy cost of walking and running at extreme uphill and downhill slopes. Journal of Applied Physiology 93, 1039–1046.

11. TSS vs. hrTSS: https://www.trainingpeaks.com/learn/articles/training-with-tss-vs-hrtss-whats-the-difference/

12. Estimating Training Stress Score: https://www.trainingpeaks.com/learn/articles/estimating-training-stress-score-tss/

13. ATL, CTL, TSB: https://www.trainingpeaks.com/coach-blog/a-coachs-guide-to-atl-ctl-tsb/

14. Peter S. Riegel: "Athletic Records and Human Endurance". American Scientist. 69: 285-290. May-June 1981

15. Hubert Beck: "Das große Buch vom Ultramarathon". Copress Sport, 2019

16. Paul Hobrough: "Running Free of Injuries". Bloomsbury Sport, 2016

17. Paul Hobrough: "The Runner's Expert Guide to Stretching". Bloomsbury Sport, 2020

APPENDIX: RUNNING POWER METERS

The following alphabetically ordered list corresponds to a selection of currently (2023) available running Power meters:

- **Apple:** In 2022, Apple added wrist-based running-Power to the Apple Watch.

- **Coros:** The watches of Coros have a wrist-based Power calculation available. Price: No additional payment is needed.

- **Garmin:** The newer generations of Garmin's sports watches come with integrated wrist-based/hybrid running Power. Price: Free.

- **Polar**: Similar to Coros, some of the newer Polar watches (Grit X and Vantage V2) come with an integrated (i.e., watch-based) Power calculation. Price: No additional fee.

- **RunPowerModel**: This is my own watch-based/hybrid solution for compatible Garmin watches. It is a data field that can be downloaded via Garmin's Connect IQ store. All the Power-meter data shown in this book were obtained with it, including the trail-score measurements. It works best in combination with a Garmin HRM-Run/Tri/Pro chest strap or Garmin run pod and watches with an integrated barometric altimeter (combination for all data here: Forerunner 945 or Fenix 6S Pro together with an HRM-Pro). Price: Free.

- stryd: As of today, this is probably the most popular running Power meter. It corresponds to an acceleration-sensor device with an integrated barometric altimeter and an on-device wind measurement. The stryd pod is attached to the shoe; all calculations are performed internally and are directly sent to the user's watch. Price: 249$

GLOSSARY

- **AP**: Average Power of a workout.
- **ATL**: Acute Training Load. Defined as the average training load in TSS per day over the last seven days.
- **cd**: Abbreviation for the cooldown phase of a workout.
- **CTL**: Chronic Training Load. Same as the ATL but using the last 6 weeks for averaging.
- **EFP**: Equivalent Flat Pace. Uses the Power output of a runner on any terrain to estimate the corresponding flat pace.
- **GAP**: Grade-Adjusted Pace. It estimates the corresponding flat pace of the runner at the same effort by correcting for the gradient.
- **IF**: Intensity Factor of a run, defined as the ratio of NP over FTP.
- **NP**: Normalized Power of a workout. Taking into account variations, it corresponds to the estimated average Power of a run with constant Power output.
- **OHR**: Optical heart rate. This is a type of heart-rate measurement, in most cases referring to wrist- and watch-based sensors.
- **RHR**: Resting heart rate. Ideally determined automatically by your sports watch when worn at night.
- **RPE**: Rating of Perceived Exertion.

- **RSC**: Running Score. Defined as the ratio of vertical to total Power in percent, it characterizes the running efficiency.
- **TIF**: Time-Corrected Intensity Factor. Compared to the IF, it takes into account the time dependency of the maximum achievable Power level.
- **TSB**: Training Stress Balance, corresponding to the difference of CTL and ATL.
- **TSC**: Trail Score. It is defined as the ratio of trail to total Power, converted to percent.
- **TSS**: Training Stress Score, quantifying the physiological load of a workout. The basis for characterizing the training load over time via the ATL and CTL.
- **VI**: Variability Index, the ratio of NP and AP.
- **wu**: Abbreviation for the warm-up phase of a workout.

Printed in Great Britain
by Amazon